100
PROJECT SUCCESS
The Right Thing for the Right Reason

100 Black Men of Atlanta Inc.

Photos from left to right above. *Row 1:* Titus D. Duncan, M.D., FACS • Alistair D. Edwards • Charles R. Edwards • Christopher R. Edwards, M.D. • Donald P. Edwards, Esq. • Stephen A. Elmore, Sr., CPA, CBA • Larry Epps • Austin O. Esogbue, Ph.D. • Leroy W. Fails • Dolan P. Falconer, Jr. *Row 2:* Darrell A. Fitzgerald, FAIA • Jesse Flanigan, III • Robert D. Flanigan, Jr. • Edsel W. Flowers • Ronald Fontenot, Esq. • Nathaniel P. Ford, Sr. • Reginald S. Fowler, M.D. • Edward M. Francis, Jr. • Ronald J. Freeman, Sr., Esq. • Sheldon L. Gathers, MBA *Row 3:* James R. Gavin, III, M.D., Ph.D. • J. Nelson Geter • Hon. Ural D. Glanville • Frank Glover, Sr., Ph.D. • Nathaniel R. Goldston, III • Nicholas G. Goodly, P.E. • Leon Goodrum • Eddie F. Grant • John T. Grant, Jr. • Keith J. Green *Row 4:* Kenneth A. Green, Sr. • Ernest L. Greer, Esq. • Ramon Gregory • Robert G. Haley • Darin C. Hall • Woodrow A. Hall • Garfield A. Hammonds, Jr. *Row 5:* Golden J. Hardy, III • Niles D. Harris • Oscar L. Harris, AIA • Sylvester J. Harris, Jr. • Gregory L. Hawkins • Dwayne E. Heard • L. Dean Heard • Paul H. Hewitt • Archibald B. Hill, III • Asa G. Hilliard, Ph.D. *Row 6:* Ernest F. Hines, Jr. • John S. Hix, Jr. • Joseph I. Hoffman, Jr., M.D. • Richard L. Holmes • Steve C. Horn • Hon. Paul L. Howard, Jr., Esq. • DeVon E. Hudson • Kenneth S. Hudson • James Mac Hunter, Esq. • Walter R. Huntley, Jr. *Row 7:* Edward D. Irons, Ph.D. • Booker T. Izell • Birdel F. Jackson, III, P.E. • Ronald Jackson • Carlos A. James • Plas T. James, M.D. • Lee A. Jenkins, Jr. • Ronnie S. Jenkins • Charles J. Johnson • Charles S. Johnson III, Esq.

Nathaniel R. Goldston, III
Founding President
(Photograph in Gold)

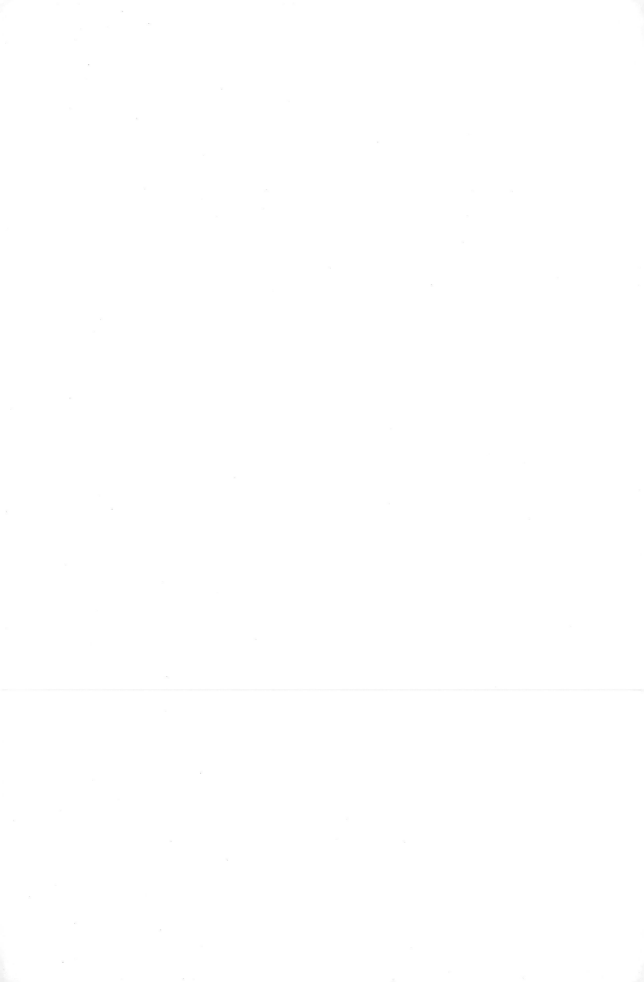

Project Success
THE RIGHT THING for the RIGHT REASON

Shelia P. Moses

Published by
100 Black Men of Atlanta, Inc.
100 Auburn Avenue N.E., Suite 301
Atlanta, Georgia 30303-2527

Book Cover design: Jones Worley Designs
Inside Design: Artwizard, Inc. and Nathan Crenshaw
Printing: ProGraphics Communications, Inc. - Charles Kelley

Research: Karen D. Roberts, Star R. Lowe, Devin D. Humphrey, Candice A. Bailey, French Thompson, Lanita D. Ward, Keldrin R. Blount, Carolyn G. Rhodes, J"Cora L. Davis, Erica M. McGinty, Shatekela L. Whitaker and Shelia P. Moses

Photo Credits: Horace Henry, Bud Smith, Benjamin Kornegay

Editors: Karen D. Roberts, Karen Heiser, Eric L. Goins, Don O'Briant

Author: Shelia P. Moses

ISBN - 0977653803

FOREWORD

Let the children speak.

Those were my thoughts when I was asked to write the foreword for this book, "The Right Thing for the Right Reason." I also thought about all the young people whose lives have been changed forever, by the grace of God and the 100 Black Men of Atlanta, Inc.

We all have had one or more life-changing experiences that we can give homage to. Joining the 100 Black Men of Atlanta, Inc. was one of those moments that changed my life. I am sure that was also the case for many of our members.

The men of the 100 will never know how many of the Archer High School students would have graduated from college, or even finished high school for that matter, if they had not been a part of Project Success. I believe it would be arrogant for us to think that we are the only reason they succeeded. We only know that in 1987, when we adopted that first class at Archer High School, they had the lowest attendance rate and the highest dropout rate in the Atlanta Public School System. The 100 Black Men of Atlanta, Inc. were extremely proud when their class graduated because thirty-two of the ninety-two students were Project Success students. Those amazing statistics tell us that there is a God looking over all of us, to whom we should give praise.

The students in Project Success often give testimonials about how this program has changed their lives. I believe their words of thanks and gratitude that come so innocently when they speak about the 100 Black Men of Atlanta. I also believe that this book is a tribute to the hard work that the students have put into this opportunity that was presented to them when they entered this program. People receive opportunities every day, but not everyone is capable of walking through the door once it is opened.

The fine young men and women in Project Success not only walked through the door, they stayed in the room. Many just needed an extra tutor and a ride to class on Saturdays. Others needed a place to live and a coat when winter came. We provided what we could, but the students did the hard part. They used their God given talents and their willpower to take the gift we offered them, and they went out and succeeded in life.

This book is filled with their life stories -- stories of hope and goodwill from the 100 Black Men of Atlanta, Inc. Stories that will let the world know that if you give our young people a chance, they can succeed.

One hundred years from now, when the history of the City of Atlanta is documented for generations to come, the stories of the students who participated in Project Success will be a part of that history. For that, the 100 Black Men of Atlanta, Inc. are proud, but we are even more proud of what the Project Success students have done.

When you read this book, I am sure that you too will be proud of our children. Please pray for them as they continue on their journey. Pray that the 100 Black Men of Atlanta, Inc. will continue to demonstrate acts of goodwill to many other children in our community in the years to come.

Congratulations to all the students who have been a part of Project Success. This book is a tribute to your hard work. Now, everyone will know that, because of you, the world is a better place.

Many Blessings,

Ambassador Andrew J. Young

ACKNOWLEDGEMENTS

We are deeply grateful to all the men, women, and children whose stories and lives made this book possible. We have all benefited from their belief that people who care can and will make meaningful differences in other people's lives.

There is no greater joy than to have people who all share a belief in a common purpose. The staff of the 100 Black Men of Atlanta, Inc. has given tirelessly of themselves to help support the efforts of our members and initiatives. Over the years we have been blessed to have some wonderful people committed to our cause. None has been more important than Monica B. Douglas, our first staff hire. Our program is what it is because she gave us our legs. Monica, we will always love you.

Special thanks are offered to all the members of the 100 Black Men of Atlanta, Inc. for your hard work, dedication and commitment. You continue to be fathers for the community and your legacies of leadership will be forever remembered. We humbly remember those whom have passed away from us. Their courage lives within us and drives our desire to continue.

There are many corporate partners to whom we are deeply grateful -- Atlanta Public Schools, The Coca-Cola Company, Georgia Power Company, Coors Brewing Company, Bank of America, Atlanta Life Financial Group, Deloitte, Delta Air Lines, Ford Motor Company, Chase Home Finance, Turner Broadcasting Systems, State Farm Insurance, The Atlanta Journal-Constitution, The Atlanta Inquirer, The Robert W. Woodruff Foundation, The Kendeda Fund, UPS, McDonald's, Tyson Foods, Verizon Wireless, the Georgia Dome, Florida A&M and Tennessee State Universities and many, many others. We have provided a complete listing in our appendix. Our partners have been the foundation upon which we were able to build our Project Success program, and for this we thank you. There are people within companies who also warrant our special thanks-- Ingrid Saunders Jones, David Ratcliffe, John Smith, Eugene Godbold, Pete McTier, Evern Cooper Epps, Phil Kent, Arthur Blank, Tom Garvey, Ervin Lee and many others who have been our friends and we appreciate you.

Along the way we have received tremendous support from the entire Atlanta community. Atlanta is one of the world's greatest cities, with the greatest people. We offer our gratitude to all of Atlanta's residents for your support and belief in our efforts.

This book would not be possible without the vision of our founding President, Nathaniel R. Goldston, III, whose vision of bringing together key African American male leaders to form this organization set in motion a chain of events that has impacted lives across this nation.

Finally, we are forever grateful to the author Shelia P. Moses who believed that this story was important enough to be told. Shelia, we could never express how much your bringing to life the stories of our students, families and members means to everyone. You are a blessing to us and we will always consider you a special part of the 100 family.

Thanks to the editors, students, photographers, and everyone who worked to bring this historical project to fruition. This has been a labor of love and we hope you will enjoy it and be motivated to make a difference.

John T. Grant, Jr.
Executive Director & Chief Operating Officer
100 Black Men of Atlanta, Inc.

*When we started the 100 Black Men of Atlanta, we knew that
God would always be Chairman of the Board.*

Nathaniel R. Goldston, III
Founding President

DEDICATION

This book is dedicated to the founding members of the 100 Black Men of Atlanta, Inc.

PROJECT SUCCESS

A PROGRAM OF 100 BLACK MEN OF ATLANTA INC.

100 100

August 8, 2005

Mr. Nathaniel R. Goldston, III
Chairman & CEO
Gourmet Services, Inc.
82 Piedmont Avenue, N.E.
Atlanta, Georgia 30303

Dear Mr. Goldston,

My name is Monica Carter and I am a Project Success Phase III and Pathways student in the Class of 2002. I am writing to say thank you for the wonderful opportunity you have provided me in the form of employment with your company at Bethune-Cookman College. I am thrilled at this chance but I must also admit I am a little nervous too, especially since you gave me a job without even a second thought as to what I could really do. This was a shock to me. I just wanted to say thank you for having faith in my abilities as a pastry chef and for taking a chance on me. I promise to do my very best to live up to the faith that you and so many other people have placed in me.

Mr. Goldston, every night I thank GOD for you and the other members of the 100 for choosing to give back to so many and for opening doors for young people like myself. I will never forget you for helping me along life's journey. You're truly one of God's greatest blessings in my life and I pray that GOD allows me to one day pass on the blessings you have given me to someone else in need.

Thankfully yours,

Monica Carter

Nathaniel R. Goldston, III
Founding President, 100 Black Men of Atlanta, Inc.
Former President, 100 Black Men of America, Inc.
President and CEO, Gourmet Services, Inc.

The 100 Black Men of Atlanta, Inc. is two hundred and sixty-six members strong. I believe our organization has tried and succeeded in making a difference in the lives of many young people in the City of Atlanta and this country. It is our hope that we will continue our mission for many years to come, and that the young men and women we serve will go out into the world and become teachers, doctors, lawyers, and leaders of their communities.

In fact, some of them have already achieved the goal of becoming strong and capable professionals. Michelle Johnson was in the first class of students selected for Project Success Phase I. She is now a senior financial analyst for the Federal Reserve of Atlanta.

Marcus Jones is a Project Success Phase III student who was one week away from being deployed to Iraq when he was interviewed for this book.

I have been deeply moved by their successes and the impact that the 100 Black Men of Atlanta have had on their lives.

Michelle F. Johnson
Project Success Phase I
Samuel H. Archer Comprehensive High School, Class of 1991
Georgia State University, Class of 1998

I had the normal life of a seven-year-old until that horrible day in 1980. On that day, in deep pain, my mother shot my father, then put the gun to her head and killed herself. So many lives were shattered at that moment.

That night, I went to live with my maternal grandmother, Frances Whitaker. Grandma lived in downtown Atlanta in the Perry Homes Housing Project. She was already an elderly lady, and raising a seven-year old girl was not in her plans for her golden years. My grandmother was warm and loving, and she was determined to put the shattered pieces of our lives back together.

She expected me to be a good girl and to receive good grades in school. We went to church together, and we shared our lives with the people in the Perry Homes community.

I loved living with my grandmother and I learned not to be afraid in the community where we lived. Yes, Perry Homes had drugs and gang violence, but the men and women in our community protected me and the other children each and every day.

When I was promoted to high school, I wanted to enroll at Frederick Douglass High School, which was located across town, instead of Archer High, which was in my school district. I was not afraid to go to Archer High, but Douglass was "the" popular high school. Douglass had a popular football and basketball program. It was exciting, and everyone wanted to be a student there.

When I told Grandma I wanted to ride the bus across town to Douglass, she looked at me and said, "Now Michelle, you can't go to Douglass. You have to go to Archer, because that school is in walking distance of Perry Homes." I tried to explain to her that I was willing to get up early to ride the bus so I would arrive at school on time. She looked at me with all the love she had and said, "I am not talking about you getting to school, I am talking about me. I have to be able to get to your PTA meetings, child. I have to be able to help you with your lessons." That's what Grandma called homework, "lessons." It was my Grandma's willingness to help me with my "lessons" that led me to Archer High School.

It was by the grace of God that Grandma could see far enough down the road to know that Archer High was where I belonged. Douglass High School was not a part of Project Success, and only at Archer would I receive the gift of being in that homeroom class the year the 100 Black Men of Atlanta chose the Project Success Phase I students.

The year after I received the gift of Project Success, I lost the gift of having my Grandma to love and guide me. She died in 1988. Though I lost her physical presence, I gained the love of my mentor and new father when God sent William "Sonny" Walker to me. Before Grandma was buried, Sonny and some of the members of the 100 Black Men of Atlanta helped me get settled into my new home with my aunt. She is a very special woman who gave me the same love that her mother had given to her. She knew how much I wanted to go

3

to college so she and Sonny did everything they could to help me enroll at Georgia Institute of Technology, where I would stay for only one year. I left college for two years, but later returned and received my degree in finance in 1998 from Georgia State University.

There were times when I felt disconnected from the world, but my aunt never gave up on me. Sonny never gave up on me. He was always there, filling in the gaps in my fatherless life. He showed me around Atlanta and showed me what it could offer a young black girl who wanted more out of life. He took me to dinners and helped me to find summer jobs. He also took me to musicals and to the theater for the first time in my life. He exposed me to everything that he thought might broaden the pictures of my life.

When I needed help, Sonny and the 100 Black Men of Atlanta, Inc. were there for me. Still, the feeling that something was missing always haunted me. Now that I am older I relate that feeling to losing my parents at such an early age. During one period of feeling this disconnection, I set out to find my father's mother, Emma Richardson.

After the death of my father, our families separated and I thought I had lost her forever. I now had the strength to face her and the loss we shared. Although she had moved away to New York after my father died, she returned to Atlanta when she retired. I remembered the street she lived on, but I did not recall her address. Somehow, I remembered her house and what it looked like from the outside. I drove up and down the street until I found my grandmother's house and I mustered up enough courage to walk up and knock on the door.

I was twenty-one years old and we had not seen each other since my parents' funeral fourteen years earlier. I was nervous to the point that I could feel myself shaking. I was looking for answers. I wanted to ask her why she didn't stay in touch with me for all those years. I wanted to know why she stopped loving me. I thought she might have blamed me in some way, or maybe I reminded her of my father too much. When she opened the door, she immediately recognized me. She hugged me and said, "Well, I was wondering when you were going to come and find me, child."

She is a short woman, and therefore when we embraced I could see over her shoulder into her living room. In that moment, all of my questions were answered without my saying one word to her. In my grandma's living room were all of my pictures from the time I was born until I was seven years old. She still loved me. She had never stopped.

After talking and hugging for the longest moment of my life, she pulled herself away from me and left the room. When she came back she sat down beside me on the couch and gave me a big box. It was filled with presents she had made for me on my birthday ever since I was seven years old. She had not forgotten me. Because of the circumstances surrounding my parents' death; I guess my grandmother did not know how I would feel about her or even how to find me. I told her that I loved her and that people had helped me when she was away. I told her my maternal grandmother was gone and my aunt had taken me in. I told her about the 100 Black Men of Atlanta. I wanted her to know that I had not lost everything when she lost her son and my mother. I was able to be a whole person in her absence and I wanted her to know that I understood her pain. I told her that together we could heal and everything was going to be all right.

Today I spend my time helping my paternal grandmother in her golden years. My son Damon has a wonderful great-grandmother to love and to love him. He talks about her as I drive him to daycare in the mornings. I smile when I drop him off and travel to the job of my dreams as a senior financial analyst for the Federal Reserve of Atlanta For me, just like Sonny promised, life is good.

My life story is just one illustration of how the 100 Black Men of Atlanta has helped young people who are struggling to find their way. The members of this wonderful organization have guided and cared for so many children like me since the inception of Project Success in 1987. I am confident that they will continue their mission for many years, and that they will, through their efforts, continue to change one life at a time.

Project Success Phase I student Michelle Johnson graduated from Archer High School in 1991. She is a 1998 graduate of Georgia State University and currently a Financial Statistics and Structure Analysis for the Federal Reserve of Atlanta.

Starting the 100 Black Men of Atlanta was an attempt to utilize individual resources collectively for the benefit of our community. It is my belief that we achieved that goal.

Joseph I. Hoffman, Jr., M.D., P.C.
Second President, 100 Black Men of Atlanta, Inc.

Marcus Jones
Project Success Phase III Student
Frederick Douglass High School, Class of 2002
Sophomore at Georgia State University (current)

My name is Marcus Jones, and I have been a member of Project Success Phase III since I was in the 4th grade. I, along with fourteen other students from William E. Boyd Elementary School, joined the program in 1992.

One of the benefits of being a Project Success student was participating in the "Read to Succeed" program. "Read to Succeed" was a volunteer committee of the 100 Black Men of Atlanta, and members would come to our school twice a month to read to the students.

I was not exposed to the world of books at that time, so "Read to Succeed" was new and exciting to me. The members of the committee assigned us two books a year to read, and they quizzed us on the content of the books to make sure we understood them. In the process, they were also challenging us to be better students, better sons and daughters, and better people.

My favorite book was entitled, "Sarah, Plain and Tall" by Patricia MacLachlan. It is a book about a girl named Sarah, who would just sit outside on her front porch and do nothing all day. One day, a man who was passing by stopped to talk to Sarah. Because he could see she was sad, he said encouraging things to her and made her feel good about herself. Sarah felt so good that she got off that porch and started doing productive things with her life.

Like Sarah, my life was also changed by a stranger, but in my case it was a whole group of them, the members of the 100 Black Men of Atlanta. I grew up in a poor neighborhood where many children never escape the crippling cycle of poverty. Many of my high school classmates aren't doing anything with their lives now, but I've been able to achieve many of my goals because the 100 Black Men of Atlanta showed me that my life did not have to imitate others. They taught me that I could go anywhere and do anything.

I have a wonderful mentor, Mr. Donald K. Murphy, who is a certified public accountant. He has always been willing to spend time with me and guide my life, like I am his own son. He's still guiding me and helping me get off the porch when he feels I have been sitting too long. One day, I want to be an accountant like Mr. Murphy.

I want to be successful like the members of the 100 Black Men of Atlanta. They have inspired me. They have inspired my entire family in a positive way. I have one sister and one brother. My brother was in a mentoring program, but nothing like Project Success. He had to drop out of Morris Brown College because of the financial situation the college has faced the past three years, but he is working hard and I know one day he will go back to school to complete his education.

If I were not being deployed to Iraq in one week, I would be enrolling as a sophomore at Georgia State University and receiving a scholarship from the 100 Black Men of Atlanta, Inc. But I signed up for the Army, and I have to see this thing through. I am a soldier and, for one year, that is what I have to be and do.

When I come back home, I will complete my studies at Georgia State University and work on my career goals. I want to join an organization one day, hopefully the 100 Black Men of Atlanta, so that I can give back to young people and return the love the 100 have given to me and many other students for almost twenty years.

But right now, I am leaving for the war. I leave next week. I don't regret signing up. I just wish I had more time. More time with my family, more time with the 100, more time with my friends, and more time just to say goodbye.

Project Success Phase III student Marcus Jones graduated from Frederick Douglass High School in 2002. He served as a member of the United States Army in Iraq for one year. Marcus is currently a sophomore at Georgia State University.

Nathaniel R. Goldston, III

As this book was being completed, Marcus Jones came home to us. I am proud to say he fulfilled his dream and returned to Georgia State University in the spring of 2005.

There are thousands of young men and women like Marcus and Michelle Johnson, who have the skills and the will to achieve amazing things if given the opportunity. The 100 Black Men of Atlanta can't save every child, but we will always strive to make a difference in the lives and futures of as many children as possible.

This was my intention in January of 1986 when I called my friend Dr. Joseph I. (Joe) Hoffman Jr. and told him about my encounter with the 100 Black Men of New York. At that time, a division of my company, Gourmet Services, Inc., was located in the Harlem State Office Building and we provided catering services for many companies and organizations that had offices there, including the 100 Black Men of New York. After a dinner we catered for the organization their president, Dr. Roscoe Lee Brown told me about the 100 Black Men of New York, and some of their founding members, including the future Mayor of New York, David Dinkins and Bruce Welling. He shared with me their mission and their goal, which was to try to address some of the negative issues that affected young people in the New York area, mainly African American men. The 100 Black Men of New York had already developed a program to further educate students in Harlem by providing scholarships to a select group of students who stayed in school and maintained at least a "C" average. The idea for this program was inspired by Eugene M. Lang, a white entrepreneur and millionaire, who promised to provide scholarships to sixty- one elementary students in Harlem if they went to college and maintained a "C" average.

Immediately, I started thinking about how good it would be if the young people in Atlanta were given the same opportunity. Mr. Lang's program had been successful and I was sure that with a lot of help from other concerned black men in my hometown we could duplicate his efforts.

Joseph I. Hoffman, Jr., M.D., P.C.
  Founding Member and Former President,
  100 Black Men of Atlanta, Inc.

No one will ever know how much Nathaniel R. Goldston, III gave of himself, his time, his company, and his financial resources to make the 100 Black Men of Atlanta, Inc. the organization it is twenty years after its inception.

I vividly recall the day Nate called me to discuss starting an Atlanta Chapter of 100 Black Men. At the time, Nate and I lived in the same neighborhood. He called me early that morning and said he wanted to stop by for a few minutes to talk about something very important. I had no idea how important it really was or that our meeting would forever change his life, my life, and the lives of hundreds of young people in the Atlanta area.

Nate excitedly told me what he had heard from Dr. Brown and others about the 100 Black Men of New York and their involvement with the local community. He shared with me his desire to duplicate and, maybe improve, their efforts right here in Atlanta. We both knew there was a great need, particularly in light of the alarming statistics that had just been released which showed that there were more African American men in this country behind bars than there were in college, that single mothers led more than fifty percent of households, and that teenage pregnancy rates were on the rise.

Like Nate, I truly believed that if we could start a chapter of the 100 Black Men in Atlanta, it would give us an opportunity to reach more young people on a larger scale than we could in our chosen professions and community service. Together, the two of us set out to make our dream a reality. That same day, Nate and I began calling a select group of black men in our community to invite them to a meeting to explore establishing an Atlanta chapter of the 100 Black Men. These men were not only our friends, they were teachers, lawyers, doctors, and other professional men that we thought were willing to go beyond writing a check a few times a year and devote their time and energy to helping improve the lives of our children.

Nathaniel R. Goldston, III

Our first meeting was held on February 4, 1986 in the Magnolia Room of the Mansion Restaurant on Piedmont Avenue. Twelve of the twenty-three men that were invited attended, including William "Bill" Campbell, Willie H. Clemons, Clarence Cooper, Alonzo A. Crim, Thomas F. Cuffie, Joseph I. Hoffman, Jr. Dwight E. Jones, Charles W. Meredith, Leon J. Oldham, Herman L. Reese, Terry J. Reynolds, George K. Robinson, Dennis Turner, Jr. , Mack Wilbourn, Edward "E.B. Williams, Robert "Bob" Williams, Charles Williams, and Walter F. Young.

We discussed all the reasons we, as African American men in the great city of Atlanta, should start a chapter. We agreed that we should join together to form a community service organization, a political force, and an economic arm of the city. We traded ideas and suggestions on what the organization's missions and goals should be, and considered assisting an existing chapter of the 100 Black Men.

Finally, we decided to create four committees: Community Programs, Political Input, Business Networking, and 100 Black Men Information Committee. The committees were charged with the responsibility of exploring in depth the ideas and suggestions that were raised at the meeting and bring back their thoughts and conclusions to the group.

We met again on February 17, 1986. One of the things we considered at that time was whether we could legally use the name, 100 Black Men. I asked Monica Douglas, who was employed at that time as an Executive Assistant at Gourmet Services, to assist us in researching this issue.

Monica B. Douglas
First Programs Director for Project Success
Research Associate, Atlanta Public Schools (current)

I was a full-time employee at Gourmet Services when Nathaniel Goldston asked me to work part-time for the 100 Black Men of Atlanta. My first task was to call Dr. Roscoe Brown to discuss the rights to using the name, 100 Black Men. Dr. Brown told me that their organization only reserved the rights to use the name "100 Black Men of New York," and therefore there was no impediment to the name being used for an Atlanta chapter.

Dr. Brown encouraged Nate and the other members to start an organization here in Atlanta. In addition to the New York chapter, there were already chapters in New Jersey, Long Island, St. Louis, Indianapolis and Los Angeles. Cincinnati was in the process of starting a chapter. Although the six chapters were formed independently with no national affiliation, they were planning a meeting for all the chapters to converge in Las Vegas on May 17th and 18th, 1986.

The members felt it was very important to attend the meeting in Las Vegas to gather information and gain a better understanding of the other chapters' goals. Therefore, they agreed to send a delegation.

Later, I contacted the Los Angeles chapter to request a copy of their by-laws to use as a guideline for forming the Atlanta chapter.

Ms. Monica Douglas addresses members of the 100 Black Men of Atlanta, Inc., and Project Success students. Behind her left to right - John T. Grant, Jr., CEO, 100 Black Men of Atlanta, Inc. and Michael Roberts, former talk show host.

Nathaniel R. Goldston, III

At our meeting on March 10, 1986, each committee presented their individual reports based upon the research they had gathered to help determine what the organization's first community project would actually be. The committee's suggestions ranged from the topic of education to a new juvenile crime task force to international projects in places as far away as South Africa.

While discussing our first project options, Dr. Alonzo A. Crim, Superintendent for Atlanta Public Schools, saw an opportunity to help further educate the young people in Atlanta and he made a suggestion that shaped the course of this organization. "I don't mean to be selfish, but why don't we begin with education. Let's start our own mentoring and tutoring program in one or more schools here in Atlanta. We can use the programs in New York as our models," he said. Everyone in the room listened when Dr. Crim spoke. We knew that we were listening to a person of high authority on the subject of education. He was known statewide for his basic philosophy that all children can learn if presented the opportunity.

We discussed his idea for the rest of the evening. Dr. Crim said he had the perfect school in mind for this program: Samuel H. Archer Comprehensive High School on Perry Boulevard in northwest Atlanta. He recommended Archer High mainly because they had some of the lowest test scores and the highest drop out rate in the entire Atlanta school system. Another reason Dr. Crim believed Archer High was the right choice for our program was because the students enrolled there mostly lived in the Perry Homes Housing Project. In 1986, Perry Homes was considered one of the worst housing developments in the state of Georgia. If any group of young people needed us, those students did.

With that information, we accepted Dr. Crim's recommendation to "adopt" Archer High School students for the program that we later named Project Success. We all agreed that we would have our new program in place by September 1986.

Dr. Crim provided guidelines for structuring the program to best meet the needs of the students. We decided that Project Success would concentrate on one homeroom class. Dr. Crim was always a fair man; therefore, after recommending that we select one homeroom freshman class, he told us that he would not decide which 8th grade class we should select. People find it hard to believe, but the first Project Success class was selected by pulling the homeroom teacher's name out of a hat. That homeroom teacher was Miss Ruth Harris, who would eventually leave Archer High and be replaced by Miss Robin Heflin.

We made a commitment to the twenty-seven original students in that class to provide them with mentoring, academic enhancement, leadership training and a post-secondary tuition assistance guarantee.

Dr. Alonzo A. Crim (deceased)
Founding member, 100 Black Men of Atlanta, Inc.
Superintendent, Atlanta Public School System

Herman L. Reese, Ed. D.
Founding Member, 100 Black Men of Atlanta, Inc. 1986
Education Committee Member
President, The Reese Group

I think about Dr. Crim a lot. We lost him in a car accident on May 3, 2000, two months after Gwendolyn, his wife of fifty years, died. Dr. Crim knew from the inception of Project Success what was needed from the 100 Black Men of Atlanta, Inc. to make the program effective. We were blessed to have this distinguished educator teach us how to help the young students at Archer High. His loyalty to educating young people and his commitment to the 100 Black Men of Atlanta, Inc. were both critical to the development of Project Success.

Dr. Crim developed Project Success only after doing a tremendous amount of research. He even talked with Eugene Lang and studied the program he started in Harlem. Dr. Crim was convinced that if black men in Atlanta could not produce a successful program similar to Dr. Lang's, it couldn't be done anywhere on this planet.

One big challenge facing Dr. Crim was that he did not pick Atlanta's most elite school or their best students. In fact, that was never his intention or desire. After seeing that Archer High's test scores were some of the lowest in the State, he knew this was the school where we should concentrate our efforts first.

Robert L. Dixon, Ph.D.
Former Principal, Samuel H. Archer Comprehensive High School
Member, 100 Black Men of Atlanta, Inc.

Like Herman, I will never forget Dr. Alonzo Crim. He was not only a fine superintendent, but a close personal friend. When he came to me in 1983, and asked me to transfer from Martin Luther King, Jr. Middle School to Archer High, I said yes because he said I was needed there to help bring the school up to standards. Not only were the test scores down, but the students had serious behavioral problems and the school itself was in bad structural condition.

Before I made a decision, I took a tour of the school and spent some time with the staff and faculty. After completing this task, I realized the conditions at Archer High were even worse than Dr. Crim thought. I went back to Dr. Crim and told him that even after my tour I would take the job if he would make me two promises: he would provide enough funding to give the school a slight makeover, and he would seek additional assistance for the children. I was particularly concerned that the students needed some type of mentoring program that would give them more guidance.

Dr. Crim was a man of his word. He immediately approved the budget to make funds available to repair the school, but help for the students did not happen as quickly. It was not because Dr. Crim was not trying. It was because you cannot write a check for someone to love our young people.

But when the opportunity came for Dr. Crim to provide help for the students he remembered his promise to me and, true to his word and character, he kept his word. After the 100 Black Men of Atlanta agreed to adopt a class to mentor and assist with their post-secondary education, Dr. Crim came directly to me.

I can still hear Dr. Crim's voice when he called and asked if I was willing to meet with the 100 Black Men of Atlanta to discuss starting a mentoring program at Archer High. He was excited about the mere possibility that these men were willing to help students who really needed them. Nate Goldston, Joe Hoffman, and Monica Douglas came to our campus to meet with Dr. Crim and me. We all became partners that day and, true to his legacy, Dr. Crim had given another child a chance to learn.

Nathaniel R. Goldston, III

Under the guidance of the Project Success Committee, Dr. Alonzo Crim, Dr. Robert Dixon, and Monica Douglas worked together with the teachers at Archer High School and brought Project Success to fruition while we finalized the incorporation of the organization. At the meeting on April 15, 1986, a motion was made and seconded to accept the by-laws that were proposed by the new By-Laws Committee. That committee included the three attorneys in the group: Judge Clarence Cooper, Thomas F. Cuffie, and Bill Campbell. Judge Cooper volunteered to serve as the chairman and agreed to start the process to incorporate our organization to become the 100 Black Men of Atlanta, Inc. We nominated and later confirmed our first official officers that night: Joseph Hoffman, Vice President; Willie Clemons, Secretary; E.B. Williams, Treasurer; Leon Oldham, Parliamentarian; Bob Williams, Chaplain; and myself as President. As the Los Angeles by-laws stated, we were all elected to serve two-year terms on the Executive Committee.

That same night, we implemented the first component under Project Success: a concept we adopted from Georgia's Gwinnett County School System. This component was designed to give any student in our program $100 if they scored 1000 or better on the Scholastic Aptitude Test (SAT).

With each new plan we envisioned for the students in Project Success, we had to consider the financial cost. We had enough men in the organization with various professional backgrounds that we could provide mentors to the young people, but we had no grasp of what we were walking into financially. We did not fully understand the cost of Project Success until we asked Jesse Hill's son-in-law Ricky Cook, who was a financial analyst with Carnegie Wealth Management Group, to provide the actual cost of sending twenty-seven students to a four-year college or university. Much to our surprise, the total cost was higher than what we imagined; $360,000 to be exact. That was $358,500 more than we had in the organization's account at that time.

The members, including myself, almost fell out of our chairs after hearing the figures Ricky presented that night. One of the members said, "What if we don't make it? We would be the biggest failure on earth." As president, I really felt that we should not give up so I addressed the members and their concerns. "Wait a minute, guys. Let's not let these numbers scare us," I said. "We can make this happen with all the resources we have as an organization. First, we call ourselves the 100 Black Men of Atlanta, Inc. with only forty members in the organization. If we can recruit one hundred members and we all agree to pay annual dues of $1,000 a year; we would have $100,000 in one year. In a period of three years, we will have $300,000 in our account." Providing actual figures to the members was helpful to ease the tension in the room. "We can also try our hand at fundraisers," I added as I tried to ensure them that everything was going to work out.

Charles "Ricky" Cook, III

Member, 100 Black Men of Atlanta, Inc.
Principal, World Leadership Group, Inc.

The $360,000 figure for the scholarships came as a shock to the men in the room. We were at Paschal's eating dinner one minute and choking on numbers the next. But I will always believe that it was that night that the 100 Black Men of Atlanta began to take themselves more seriously.

Everything changed when the fact that we were truly responsible for raising such a large amount of money became a reality. The good news is I believe that the 100 truly stepped up to the plate and did what had to be done to financially secure the education of those twenty-seven students who otherwise may not have had a chance.

Nathaniel R. Goldston, III

After Ricky had completed his report, I turned to Leon Oldham, who was chair of the fundraising committee at the time, and asked him to research probable fundraising ideas. He suggested that we have a major dinner with a well-known entertainer to help us raise the money needed for Project Success.

Dr. Willie Clemons was also in attendance that night, and everyone in Atlanta knows that if you want an affair arranged in the proper manner, he's the person you call. For years, Dr. Clemons had co-chaired the Mayor's Masked Ball with Mrs. Billye Aaron, raising thousands of dollars for the United Negro College Fund. We were delighted when he agreed to coordinate and chair our first social fundraiser.

While the social committee planned the fundraiser, the Atlanta chapter was chosen to host the 1987 Annual Convention for the 100 Black Men of America. The six chapters had met in May, 1986 in Las Vegas, and again in September of that year at the Congressional Black Caucus meeting in Washington, D.C. where we discussed incorporating and uniting all the chapters.

The 100 Black Men of America held a follow-up meeting on October 3, 1986 in Washington, D.C., and William Hayling of the New Jersey chapter presided over the meeting. At that meeting, the 100 Black Men of America was incorporated as a holding company and the members decided that each chapter of the organization would thereafter be known as the 100 Black Men of (the respective city where they were located), Inc. A committee was also formed at that meeting to develop the new national by-laws. The first officers for 100 Black Men of America, Inc. were William Hayling, President; Oliver Lofton, Vice President; Moses Gray, Secretary; and Jesse Swanigan, Treasurer.

We were excited about holding the national convention in Atlanta. It would give everyone an opportunity to meet the new officers and learn more about the programs the individual chapters already had in place.

In addition to coordinating workshops, meetings, and panel discussions, we needed entertainment for the large number of guests we were expecting. The motion was made and carried that the social committee would plan our first fundraising event around the National Convention.

Willie H. Clemons, Ph. D.

Founding Member and Chair of Special Events,
100 Black Men of Atlanta, Inc.
Associate Vice President at Morehouse School of Medicine

When Nate asked me to become a founding member of the 100 Black Men of Atlanta, Inc., I answered him with a question, "Why me?" I asked that because most of the organizations I was affiliated with were related to education, such as the Mayor's Masked Ball, a fundraiser for the United Negro College Fund. Because Nate and I have been friends for over twenty years, I was willing to help him in any way I could.

Just listening to Nate's excitement made me excited about becoming a member. I knew that the 100 Black Men of Atlanta, Inc. was going to be different than any other organization in Atlanta. After becoming a member, I joined the Education Committee, which later was renamed the Project Success Committee. But my primary responsibility was, and remains to date, serving as chairman for our first fundraising, which we named Le Cabaret.

Nate told me that he felt I would bring the expertise to help the 100 Black Men of Atlanta; Inc. set the tone for their social functions for fundraising. He made it clear to me that, like the United Negro College Fund, the 100 Black Men of Atlanta's mission is to help enrich the lives of young people by providing them with a post-secondary education. That was the key element for me to join this organization and to serve as chair for Le Cabaret for nineteen years.

After celebrating our first social function, a Christmas party at Joe and Pam Hoffman's home in December of 1986, I started the New Year planning Le Cabaret for the National Convention with the help of Sonia Young and Pam Hoffman of Eventions, Inc, a special events management company in Atlanta. The National Convention was a success. Our beloved member and former mayor of Atlanta, Maynard H. Jackson, served as keynote speaker during the opening session on Friday May 22, 1987 at the first President's Luncheon. Renowned author, Alex Haley, was our special guest.

Former Mayor of Atlanta and member Maynard H. Jackson (deceased) speaking at luncheon for the First Annual National Convention for the 100 Black Men of America at the Westin Peachtree Plaza Hotel, Atlanta, Georgia, May 22, 1987.

Author, Alex P. Haley (deceased) speaking at luncheon for the First Annual National Convention for the 100 Black Men of America at the Westin Peachtree Plaza Hotel, Atlanta, Georgia, May 22, 1987.

Dr. Willie H. Clemons

On Saturday, May 23, 1987, we held our first Le Cabaret at the Westin Peachtree Plaza Hotel. Singer Phyllis Hyman was our featured entertainer.

I would be the first to tell you that we were tested in every way on the day we prepared for the first Le Cabaret. Many musicians will only take cash payments for their performance. On the day of Le Cabaret, we learned that Ms. Hyman had the same policy in her contract, but we had inadvertently overlooked it. To make matters worse, it was Saturday, and most banks were closed. One of our members, Leon Goodrum, drove all over Atlanta to the different McDonald's restaurants he owned replacing his cash drawers with checks from members of the 100. The members went to ATM machines to get money, and some of us probably broke into a few of our children's piggy banks until we had $15,000 cash in hand for Ms. Hyman.

Every member who was involved in Le Cabaret pulled together using whatever resources and connections we had until we met the financial obligations for the event. I knew that day we were going to succeed as an organization because we were truly committed.

Prior to the convention and LeCabaret, we held a press conference on April 30, 1997 to announce Project Success. We had given the community our word to support the students at Archer High School, and we intended to keep it. That desire kept us going as we worked tirelessly to make sure that the convention and LeCabaret were a success.

The people of the City of Atlanta came out in full support of our organization on the night Le Cabaret was held. There was not an empty seat in the house. The event raised $65,000 for Project Success, and helped us introduce our new program and our new organization to the City of Atlanta. I cannot tell you how encouraged we were the next day when we tallied up the figures, and recalled the great time everyone had shared.

Singer, Phyllis Hyman (deceased) performed at the First Le Cabaret during 1987 National Convention, for 100 Black Men of America. Westin Peachtree Plaza Hotel. May 23, 1987

Members of the 100 Black Men of Atlanta, Inc. attend the first Le Cabaret, Westin Peachtree Plaza Hotel. May 23, 1987

Dr. Willie H. Clemons

The success of our first Le Cabaret was truly astonishing because we did not have the level of corporate support that we have today. Anheuser-Busch Companies donated $5,000, Rich's provided the decorations, and Georgia Power Company printed the invitations. We succeeded because of the hard work of a small group of dedicated men and the support of the people of the City of Atlanta. After what we accomplished with the first Le Cabaret, we knew that we could raise whatever money we needed to keep our commitment to the students of Project Success.

Following Le Cabaret, we used the summer months to get better acquainted with each other, the Project Success Students, and their parents. One of the ways we did this was by having a picnic on July 11th at Clarence Duncan Memorial Park in. We invited all of the students, teachers, and parents to attend. During the summer, we also asked the students and parents to sign a covenant agreement to reinforce their commitment to Project Success.

Project Success Phase I students on a field trip. (Left to right: Alicia Almond, Alphia Stephens, Tameka Brown, and Sonya Jelks.)

Dr. Willie H. Clemons

I was very excited about getting to know my new mentee, Pamela Lewis. Pamela is a wonderful young woman from the Perry Homes community who has suffered and overcome many hardships in her life. Her mother was a drug addict and her father was absent from her life, so she was not sure about me or anyone else in the organization in the beginning stages. To our advantage, she was only one year younger than my oldest daughter Lybra, and they became good friends.

A very important part of our mentoring program is the support we receive from our own families. You cannot walk in the door and say the student you're mentoring is a part of the family. You have to ask your family for their love and support.

My family was with me one hundred per cent when I began mentoring Pam. I'm sure my daughters laugh when they think about how quickly our family changed from a family of four to a family of five as we began to treat Pam as one of our own. I applaud my daughters, Lybra and Lailee, along with my wife, Leteria, for adapting to our new family member, and I appreciate my children's willingness to share Mommy and Daddy.

Pamela eventually enrolled at Hampton University in Virginia. She graduated with a B.S. degree in English and Early Childhood Education in 1996. I am proud to say she is presently a teacher at Anderson Parks Elementary School in Atlanta, and she was named teacher of the year in 2002. Pam's story is one of many that we are proud to share. We are proud to say she beat the odds.

The Project Success program provides a beacon of light in the darkness.

Dr. L. Vernon Allwood
Assistant Professor
Morehouse School of Medicine

THE RIGHT THING for the RIGHT REASON

Nathaniel R. Goldston, III

By the fall of 1987, Ms. Douglas, Dr. Dixon, and Ms. Heflin had developed a system for our members to help the students at Archer High School with tutoring, weekend trips, and financial support, if needed. We had no manual. We just knew that together we could make these young people's lives better than their present situation.

Dr. Crim decided to conduct a workshop to help us become better mentors, which he entitled "How to be a Mentor." We were all required to attend, and it proved to be very helpful. For some of us, it was the first time that we had served as mentors and we found it to be challenging. With guidance from Dr. Crim and Dr. Dixon, our mentors began to develop the skills they needed to help the Project Success students. We worked hard with our mentees, but it did not take us long to understand that we could not meet all their needs and the growing demands of the organization relying solely on volunteers. Therefore, we hired Monica Douglas to serve as the full time director of Project Success. Because Dr. Crim was so knowledgeable of the one-on-one needs of the students, he made it possible for Ms. Douglas to have an on-site office at Archer High School. This gave the students daily access to Monica and gave her the opportunity to get to know each and every one of them.

As mentors, we quickly learned that when you "adopt" the child you "adopt" the whole family. Most of the students were from single- family homes headed by mothers, and they received very little support from their fathers. Most of the mothers welcomed our helping their children with open arms. I remember one mother telling me that she knew God had sent the 100 Black Men of Atlanta, Inc. to her. She said that we were their guardian angels. To hear her say those words made me feel good as a mentor and as a man because we really were working with these young people from the heart.

When I say the words "from the heart," I know that I speak for the majority of our members because we all committed ourselves to the students and the goals we had set for them despite the challenges and obstacles we had to overcome. I remember going into Perry Homes to pick up my mentee, Antonio Thomas for the first time. The Perry Homes community was considered a rough neighborhood and many people in Atlanta were afraid to drive down the streets in that area. Honestly, I was not afraid because I grew up in one of the roughest projects in St. Louis, Missouri. Because of my own experience I knew that no matter where you live, you deserve the opportunity to better yourself.

The young men in Perry Homes, who had no association whatsoever with the 100 Black Men of Atlanta, Inc., welcomed us to their community. They would stand on the corner and say, "Don't mess with him, that's Mr. Goldston. He is here to pick up Tony." I did not feel threatened by them in any way and they would even guard my car when I went inside Tony's apartment to pick him up. Most of them were children like Tony and they just needed someone to give them a chance. Young people know when adults care about them. I just wish I could have helped more of those young people who looked in my eyes when I went to pick Tony up. Every time I left Perry Homes, that same thought raced

31

through my head.

I felt like a proud father the day Tony graduated from Archer High School. I felt the same way when he went off to college at Grambling University that fall. Tony was a great athlete, but he did not play football the first year because we wanted him to focus on his grades. He did well academically and played football his sophomore year. His plans for college and professional football were altered during his junior year when he became a father. Tony made the decision to leave college, marry, and support his family. As much as I wanted Tony to graduate from Grambling, I respect him for his decision to be there for his new wife and child. Now, he has a wonderful wife, a son and he is a productive member of society in every way that matters.

Not every child's journey from that class at Archer High School has been as successful as Tony's, but we have collectively tried to give them every opportunity that we can.

Monica B. Douglas

I will always believe that Dr. Crim's ability to provide an office for me at Archer High School changed the course of Project Success. From the point I located to the campus, the students had daily access to the 100 Black Men of Atlanta as an organization and to me, as a representative and agent of their mentors.

Dr. Crim's wisdom in providing this type of on-site access gave me a new perspective of what the students' lives were really like. They came from various backgrounds, and that required us to treat each student's situation directly and individually. Not only were many fathers absent from the homes, in some cases older siblings were raising their younger sisters and brothers, many students like Michelle Johnson lived with their grandparents. Some students and parents did not welcome the members or me with open arms in the beginning, and that made it difficult to know what they really needed for at least the first six months of the program. These young people had not had the advantages in life that some members and I had growing up, but they were not stupid. We had to prove to them that we were sincere in our intentions toward them just as they had to prove to us that they were committed to the program.

I began to truly understand the reasons for the students' and parents' reservation when Dr. Dixon sat me down in his office one day and explained that in the past other organizations had come into Perry Homes and Archer High School and made false promises. As a result, some of the students felt they had been used as guinea pigs for press conferences until the cameras were off. Once the press left, the students felt they were forgotten.

The information Dr. Dixon shared with me made me realize that the students were not going to come to my office and simply start talking. I would have to go to them, and that is exactly what I did. With permission from Dr. Dixon and the parents, I arranged to visit each student in their home. After my initial visits, I saw a big improvement in the communication between the students. Somehow, the fact that I had taken the time to go to their homes, places where most people were afraid to go, meant so much to them. Within weeks of the visits, the students were stopping by my office just to say hello. Their sweet hellos soon turn into long conversations about their classes, their families and friends, and life in general. They realized that I was there to assure them that everything was going to work out between them and their mentors. I was the voice of the 100 for them, and also a sounding board.

Eventually, I found myself teaching the members about the students. One of the first things I learned was that no matter how difficult the students' lives may have appeared to us, they did not see their situation as being that bad. The fact that they didn't have money did not mean they did not have some of the things they needed, including self-esteem. Some students did not feel they needed "saving" at all, and that took a while for some members to realize. I had to tell them as frankly as I could that they were not knights on white horses to these children, but that they could still make a difference in their lives.

Dr. Robert L. Dixon

One of the wonderful and strange things that happened at Archer High when the 100 Black Men of Atlanta adopted those twenty-seven students was that the other students who were not a part of Project Success also began to evolve. They felt they should show the students in Project Success that they too could be successful. If jealousy was ever used in a positive manner, this was an example. A very good one. Before I knew it, the students whom teachers considered at risk were doing better academically and socially. There were students who were not in Miss Heflin's homeroom class going to Monica's office to ask her if they could join Project Success.

Many students became the keepers of the gate at Archer High School. They wanted to improve what was once a bad reputation. The press had always written about Archer High and Perry Homes, but the articles were mostly about fights and gun violence, not the students' good grades. Now, they were writing about Project Success and the overall involvement of the students at Archer High.

The students did not want to be in trouble, and they did not want to be around trouble makers. They saw themselves in a positive light and they were seriously trying to protect that image. The change in these students made all of us feel good because we could see they were looking toward their bright futures.

There was one particular incident that made me realize that Project Success had truly impacted the entire student body at Archer High. One day, a student brought a homemade bomb to school and caused a small fire in the hallway. I was so angry that I called every student, teacher, and faculty member into the school auditorium to discuss the. I wanted to know who had done such a foolish thing. I had always left the door open for my students to tell me when there was a problem in the school without their feeling I would reveal the source. That day, I explained to the students the seriousness of having a bomb in the school and I promised them that I would not reveal the student's name if someone came forth with information about who started the fire. As the students were leaving the auditorium, I felt someone slip a piece of paper into the palm of my hand. On the paper was the name of the student who had actually made the bomb. When we started looking for him, we found him in the nurse's office pretending he was sick from smoke inhalation. After talking to the student for a long time, I learned he had set the bomb off to get attention. What he did not understand was that other students wanted attention too, but they wanted it for positive actions, not negative ones.

I learned that day that anyone can change if given enough love and attention. When they change, they no longer want to be around negative people. The students finally understood that it was more important to receive attention for their good deeds than bad.

After that incident, I started to stress to the students even more than ever how fortunate they were to have the 100 in their lives. I told them how special they were and how much the teachers and the 100 cared about them. It took them a moment to realize that, out of all the students in the City of Atlanta, they were the chosen ones.

Dr. Robert L. Dixon, Sr., past principal at Samuel H. Archer High School and 100 member, spends time with his mentee Monica Carter. Monica graduated from the Florida Culinary Institute in 2005.

Sonya Jelks
Project Success Phase I
Samuel H. Archer High School, Class of 1991
Syracuse University, Class of 1997
Currently Project Manager, EDI Specialist at the Phillips Company

When I think about how I became part of Project Success, I know that I was chosen by God. I had only been enrolled at Archer High School for about ten days when my homeroom class was selected by the 100 Black Men of Atlanta, Inc. In addition to being a new student at Archer High, my newly-divorced mother, with my two sisters and me in tow, had just relocated to Atlanta. The odds of being in that class can only come from God's grace. I was not living in Perry Homes like many of my classmates, but the lifestyle I knew when my parents were together was gone.

The first indication that Project Success was going to work for me was Miss Monica Douglas. I cannot explain how it felt to see her every day, caring and loving us the way she did.

The females were more comfortable talking to Miss Monica than we were to the male members for a very long time. So I put my trust in her and hoped that everything they were telling us was true. I was not sure how any of this was going to work out, but I knew that I had always wanted to go to college and they were promising to pay my full tuition. I knew that for thirteen years I had lived with my daddy and now he was not with us. The thought of these men spending time with me made me happy, because I missed daddy.

My father is a good man, but I had to adjust to his being my daddy without his being my mother's husband. God was watching over me because he sent not one but two good men to be my mentors and friends. They were Bernard M. Porché and Howard J. Spiller, who have totally different but wonderful personalities. I was fortunate enough to have parents who welcomed the love and support from both of my mentors.

Former President of 100 Black Men of Atlanta, Inc., Bernard M. Porché and his mentee Sonya Jelks, attend the President's Luncheon at the Omni Hotel in Atlanta, Georgia on June 10, 1989.

Howard J. Spiller
Board Member, 100 Black Men of Atlanta, Inc.
President, H.J.S. and Associates/Urban Resources

I am so proud of Sonya. From the first time I met her, I knew she was special. I always knew she would do well in life. She had such character and grace, even as a young child.

When the members began spending time with the students, we asked them "What do you want to be when you grow up?" They had little or no aspirations at the time. Every child in the room named a blue collar job, except one person.

I have nothing against the way a man feeds his family, but I thought it was heartbreaking that out of twenty-seven students only one mentioned a career that required some form of post-secondary education. Sonya was that student. She raised her precious hand and said, "I want to be a secretary."

That was a small indication that Sonya's dreams for herself were a little more than those around her. I did not see her as different from the other students, but I just knew she would be a leader in Project Success.

Sonya Jelks

It was always easy to have a heart-to-heart conversation with Mr. Spiller. We spent a lot of Sunday afternoons just riding around the city talking about life. He cares about people. He cared about what happened to me.

So many summers when I needed a job, he was right there to help me get in the door, and he stayed in contact with me to make sure that I got all that I needed to succeed in the place where I was employed.

As much as Howard and Bernard differ, they had the same common goal for me. They both wanted me to go to college and to do well in life.

Bernard M. Porché
Vice President for Management and Strategic Initiative
B and E Jackson and Associates

I was fortunate enough to be in the first group of men inducted into the 100 Black Men of Atlanta, Inc. after the founding members established the organization, and I was also fortunate enough to have Sonya as my mentee. She has been a part of my life and my family's life for eighteen years now.

Sonya's background was somewhat different from most of the students in Project Success because she was not a native Atlantan and she had not grown up in Perry Homes. What she did have in common with her classmates was the need for help in areas that her parents could not provide at the time.

Sonya was willing to learn and, after a few months, she was excited about being a part of Project Success. However, in the beginning, she wanted to make sure that the 100 Black Men were not going to just ride in on our white horses and leave after the cameras were turned off. She had heard rumors about different organizations choosing inner-city students like her as their mentees and making them false promises. Those promises were sometimes short lived and the students sometimes never saw the mentor again. Some students at Archer High had experienced that as well, and they made it known to the other students.

Sonya was smart and, in an almost funny way, made it clear that we were not going to use her. She knew what she wanted out of life and she made it clear that we had to show her that we were sincere. It took time, but I eventually proved to her that I was truly interested in her education and her overall well-being. My family also helped build the relationship between Sonya and me. My wife, Bobbie, and our four children liked her immediately, and Sonya knew it.

I will never forget the day Sonya called us and said, "I think I want to do this Project Success thing if you make me one promise."

"And what promise is that?" I asked.

"Well, I want you to promise me that you are going to hang in there and not leave me the way the children at school are saying you are going to do."

I promised her that we would be with her until the end.

I cried when I hung up the telephone because I knew Sonya's life and my life would never be the same. They weren't.

The 100 Black Men of Atlanta took a risk on making hundreds of inner-city students productive citizens when no one, not even the students themselves believed it could happen.

Ingrid Saunders Jones
Senior Vice President, Corporate External Affairs
The Coca-Cola Company and Chairperson,
The Coca-Cola Foundation

Monica B. Douglas

I could see the change in the Project Success students as they began to develop secure relationships with their mentors. The first few months were a series of learning curves for the mentors and the mentees, but eventually they grew together.

It was very important for the mentors to see the world through the same eyes that the children saw it. It was important to me that the mentors saw what the students saw daily. To achieve that goal, I moved the meetings between members and students to Archer High School. The students had to walk to school through the problems that occurred in Perry Homes every day. If they could do that, the members could drive through those same streets a few times a month. It was a good and humbling experience for the members to experience what their mentees experience every single day of their young lives.

To further involve the members in the students' lives, we adopted a policy that stated the students would no longer catch the bus to their mentors' homes. Like Nate had always done, the mentors now had to pick the students up from Perry Homes. The new policy, along with the members' visiting parents and my presence at Archer High, allowed the members to really get to know and understand each child's individual needs. Simply by driving to the students' homes, the members were learning not just who the students were, but also where they came from. I believed that if the members could understand where the children came from, they could understand where they were going. More importantly, the 100 could understand how to help them get there.

Not all of the students' situations were as bad as we thought. Some members were surprised to learn that some of the children's parents were well educated, but had fallen on hard times. They also learned that although their circumstances were poor, many had their own hopes and visions.

It was also a wake-up call for the members to realize that the children did not see themselves as desperate and poor. Realizing this helped the members in the way they approached the students. Whatever the students' conditions were at home or at school, the members always made it clear that they were not knights on shining white horses. They were simply men who cared.

Nathaniel R. Goldston, III

We will never be able to thank Monica enough for what she brought to the table as the first Program Director for Project Success. Just having her at Archer High each day gave the members a whole different perspective of what the students were experiencing. She was instrumental in helping us evaluate the individual needs of each student.

Within a few months after we started the program, our Project Success students were calling us the "100 Black Dudes" and calling Monica, "Momma." In no way did we view our new nicknames as disrespectful. We all saw this as a sign of comfort for the students.

As we worked through those initial hurdles of getting Project Success off the ground, we continued to focus on the financial obligations we had made to them. One of the requirements we have always looked for when recruiting new members was their ability to help in an area that is beneficial to children in the Project Success.

Many members had strong corporate connections, and we asked them to use those relationships to solicit money for Project Success. We were in the process of writing letters to potential corporations requesting donations when I received a call from the late Dillard Munford. Dillard was a board member for the Gannett Foundation and the owner of a chain of Majik Markets convenience stores throughout Atlanta. He had just read an article in the Atlanta Journal Constitution about Project Success when he phoned my office. He had already discussed wanting to assist the 100 Black Men of Atlanta, Inc. with WXIA-TV vice president, Sheryl Gripper, and he asked her to join us in a meeting.

Sheryl Gripper
Vice President of Community Affairs, WXIA-TV
11 Alive News

Most African Americans would have been insulted by what Mr. Munford said to Mr. Goldston, Dr. Hoffman, and me, but I think he was just being honest.

"Nate, the 100 Black Men of Atlanta is the first group of black folks I have ever seen trying to help themselves. I like what I read in the Atlanta Journal. Would you and your organization be interested in taking some money from some white folks?" he said.

We were a bit taken aback by his frankness, but after we got over the shock, Nate, in his classic spirit of kindness, said, "I don't see why not." Nate was not thinking about himself, he was thinking about the young people who needed help. He has never compromised himself or the members, he just understands people.

As a Gannett Foundation board member, Mr. Munford was planning to ask them to donate $50,000 to the 100 Black Men of Atlanta, Inc. for Project Success. This money would be paid in two installments of $25,000 over a two-year period.

Nathaniel R. Goldston, III

What Dillard Munford said about black people not helping themselves was not true then, and it is not true today. That was simply his opinion and maybe the opinion of many other white people from his era. Black people have been trying to help themselves since they were brought to America six hundred years ago. Every element from racism to lack of education has stood in our way as a race. Time has passed and we are on a different playing field now. People can always help themselves when you level out the playing fields and everyone is playing by the same rules.

In Dillard Munford's heart, he knew that was true and, I believe, that was the reason he called us. That was the reason he wanted to help. I told Sheryl and Joe when we left that meeting, "You know, whenever you do the right thing for the right reason, you are going to be successful."

Dillard Munford kept his word to us and in October 1987, the 100 Black Men of Atlanta, Inc. received the first installment of $25,000 from the Gannett Foundation in the form of stock that we could transfer to money at our discretion. The second installment would follow in May of 1988.

After receiving the first check from the Gannett Foundation, we began to receive responses from the other corporations that the members had contacted. In 1988, Adolph Coors Brewing Company Vice President, Ivan Burwell, graciously donated $25,000.

Even with the growing support from corporations, we knew that proceeds from Le Cabaret were simply not going to be enough to pay tuition for twenty-seven students. On January 12, 1988, the Fundraising Committee introduced a new idea to the members. They had been charged with the task of finding a new fundraiser that would generate a profit of $150,000 or more to help cover the expenses for Project Success.

Chairman Leon Oldham suggested the 100 Black Men of Atlanta, Inc. use football as a mechanism for raising money. He told us about the football game he had attended for the last fifteen years between his alma mater Tennessee State University and Florida A&M University.

Leon J. Oldham
Founding and Former Member, 100 Black Men of Atlanta, Inc.

I stood up at that meeting and said, "We need to bring Florida A&M and Tennessee State to Atlanta for a football game."

Confused, everybody looked at me and said, "Why?"

I laughed and said, "Because a game between those two rival teams would mean over $100,000 in revenue for us."

Every time FAMU plays Tennessee State away from Florida, they have an average of 18,000 people from that State who follow them wherever they are going. When Tennessee plays FAMU away from Tennessee, guess what? Their fans travel to that game. That means 36,000 tickets are sold before the box office even opens.

Nathaniel R. Goldston, III

While Dr. Clemons finalized the plans for the second Le Cabaret, Leon and his committee focused on planning the first football game for the fall of 1989. We all agreed that the next fundraiser we had would be called the Ebony Classic, and it would become an annual event.

It did not take us long to realize what Leon already knew about black college football: the games between rival teams are about more than football. There are also the battle of the bands, the parties, and all sorts of events that the fans travel from all over the country to participate in each year.

Dr. Willie H. Clemons

With the success of the first Le Cabaret in 1987, and the growing number of tables sold, we had no choice but to move the 1988 Le Cabaret to the Georgia World Congress Center. With former Miss America, Suzette Charles, as our entertainment, Le Cabaret 1988 was a huge success with 1,100 people in attendance. The accounts receivable for that evening totaled $153,600. After deducting our expenses, we had netted $90,000 for the Project Success Program.

To top the evening off we were below budget by approximately $1,600.

We were overwhelmed and delighted by the support we received from the people of Atlanta. They recognized that the 100 Black Men of Atlanta were working for the good of our students and they were willing to help by simply buying a ticket.

We began to receive recognition from the press, and that same year The Children's Defense Fund selected Project Success as one of three model programs in the Atlanta area. The good news of Project Success apparently reached New York City, because Tony Brown, host of The Tony Brown Journal, called upon us to host the Atlanta viewing of his new PG-13 film production, "White Girl."

Like Mr. Brown's show, "White Girl" was a powerful documentary focusing on drugs and how they affect our community. We decided that "White Girl" was a "must see" for our students, and we also designed it as a fundraiser for organizations like the 100 Black Men of Atlanta. It was as simple as getting the community involved and selling tickets with the proceeds to be divided between the organization and Tony Brown Productions.

Because I was working on Le Cabaret III, I recommended that one of our newest members, John T. Grant, Jr. chair the preview of "White Girl." I was John's sponsor when he joined the organization, and I felt he was perfect for the assignment. John was only twenty-eight years old when I met him. He served our organization as a volunteer for two years until he was old enough to join. He was hard working and reliable, and during that time he showed the same fortitude that existed in the founding members. Given John's many talents, it is no surprise that he eventually became the Executive Director and Chief Operating Officer of the 100 Black Men of Atlanta.

John T. Grant, Jr., Executive Director
Chief Operating Officer, 100 Black Men of Atlanta, Inc.

The premier of Tony Brown's film, "White Girl" was a new and refreshing experience in Atlanta.

In addition to sponsoring the premiere, we organized a panel discussion conducted by our member and noted psychiatrist Lloyd T. Baccus, M.D., which was held at the Georgia Pacific Corporation auditorium the day before the movie was shown. Along with our Project Success students, we bused in 254 additional students from Atlanta Public Schools to see the film.

Following the screening, the students held a debate to discuss the film and the effect drugs have on young people and their communities. The gathering was provocative and enlightening for everyone in attendance.

"IT HAS A POWERFUL ANTI-DRUG THEME."
-Donna Britt,
USA TODAY

"TONY BROWN IS ABOUT TO GIVE ALL OF
AMERICA A ZOOPER FIRST-CLASS MOVIE"
-Jack The Rapps

"THIS FILM HAS THE POTENTIAL FOR
GAINING MORE CRITICAL ACCLAIM
THAN ANYTHING I HAVE DONE
SINCE *ROOTS*."
-Joseph Wilcots
Director of Photography

A TONY BROWN FILM

THE WHITE GIRL

A BREAKTHROUGH MOVIE

A TONY BROWN PRODUCTION THE WHITE GIRL
TROY BEYER · TAIMAK · TERESA FARLEY
DIANNE SHAW · O.L. DUKE · PETRONIA PALEY · DONALD CRAIG
Executive Producer SHERYL CANNADY Producer JIM CANNADY
Director of Photography JOSEPH M. WILCOTS
Written and Directed by TONY BROWN

A love story
of danger in a
changing world.

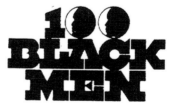

100 Black Men of Atlanta, Inc.
Robert W. Woodruff Arts Center
Symphony Hall
November 11, 1988
8:30 P.M.

50

Dr. Joseph I. Hoffman, Jr.

In 1989, I became president of 100 Black Men of Atlanta. My number one priority was to continue Nate's legacy and his loyalty to the organization, to Project Success, and to the community.

To accomplish this, I held a meeting with Monica Douglas and John Grant to receive a first hand report on the students' progress at Archer High School. At the beginning of the meeting, John and Monica made it clear that the money we were raising to send the students to college would not be needed unless the students' grades improved.

John T. Grant, Jr.

When I was asked to chair the Project Success Program, my first act was to assess the status of our students in Project Success. I asked one of our members, Dr. Norman J. Johnson, who was Assistant to President Pat Crecine at Georgia Tech at the time, to meet with me because he was an educator. Dr. Johnson told me that the three elements needed to evaluate the level of our students' progress were grade point averages, attendance rates, and conduct.

I immediately went to the organization and requested that we make a financial investment to have all of the Project Success students evaluated by the Southwest Achievement Center. When the scores came back, they showed that our Project Success students would be graduating in two years, but that eighty percent of them were not prepared to take the SAT. Their grade point averages were decreasing, their absentee rates were increasing, and some of them were again showing signs of poor conduct.

Monica and I explained to Dr. Hoffman that the afternoon tutoring we were providing would no longer be enough to prepare the Project Success students for the SAT or to help them bring their grades up to standard. Based upon our new findings, we suggested a sixth day of school to help the students achieve their academic goals.

Dr. Joseph I. Hoffman, Jr.

At our meeting, Monica and John suggested that we consider offering a Saturday Academy for the Project Success student. The Academy would cost our organization at least $150,000 for the remainder of the time the students had left in high school. At the time, we had $360,000 in our account. That was just enough to pay the full tuition for all twenty-seven of the students if they went to college.

The solution was simple and difficult all at the same time: we needed more money. We started to focus on the success of the upcoming football classic as a possible solution to pay for the Saturday Academy.

Monica B. Douglas

I felt confident that Joe and the other members would find a way to fund the Saturday Academy to ensure that the students in Project Success would get a college education. Once the academy was financed, we knew we had to find a way to get the students to attend. We were still struggling with some of them attending their regular classes. How on earth were we going to get them in a Saturday class?

John Grant, who was Chairman of the Project Success Committee, and I immediately called a meeting to tell the students they would now be required to attend class on Saturdays. When talking to the students, we usually did so in their homeroom class, where they were comfortable. Ninety percent of the time a member would come in and provide the information they needed and I would be there to help the students adjust and answer any questions they might have. John Grant coming into their homeroom and telling them that they were required to attend Saturday classes was a major blow to a few of the students, but it was necessary.

John T. Grant, Jr.

I will never forget the day I told the class they were required to go to school every Saturday until one o'clock. I was very clear when I said, "Over there is the door. If you are not willing to go to class on Saturday, that door has a knob on only one side. If you walk out there is no knob to let you walk back in." Two students got out of their seats and walked out of the classroom. I did not try to stop them because I felt that we had gone the distance with these young people and they knew we were not going to abandon them now.

We assured the students that we would help them with this transition. This was important because ninety-five percent of them were living below the poverty line. Their families' financial situation required some of them to hold weekend jobs to help their parents pay the utility bills, not to buy themselves a pair of sneakers.

We knew who had jobs, where they worked, and how much money they made each Saturday. We knew we couldn't and shouldn't just walk in that classroom and say, "You are going to class." Instead, we told each student before they were given the option of leaving that they would be given a check for that same amount of money they earned each Saturday.

We found a solution for any excuse the students offered for not being able to attend the Saturday Academy. Our members even went out and talked to the students' employers. They explained that the students had to attend school on Saturdays and therefore could no longer work that day.

I do not know where those two students are who walked out the door that day. I hope that they succeeded in life without our help. I only know that the 100 Black Men of Atlanta gave them a chance.

Dr. Joseph I. Hoffman, Jr.

It was clear from day one that John Grant was going to be a leader in this organization after the success of "White Girl." So clear that President-Elect Charles Meredith appointed him as Chairman of the Project Success Committee. Because we had such confidence in John, we supported the way he walked in that room and gave the students an ultimatum. "This is it, guys. The two students, who got up and left, did so on their own accord. They did not leave for any other reason," he said. The students understood him, and thankfully most of them decided to stay.

By Le Cabaret III, Dr. Clemons and his committee had the event down to a science. A sold out crowd enjoyed a wonderful evening with singer Angela Bofill. Our annual President's Luncheon was also well attended that year, with General Colin Powell as the keynote speaker.

Unfortunately, the planning and implementing of the football game was not going as well. We were at a board meeting seventy-two days away from the Classic when the committee realized we were in trouble.

This was a new fundraiser that did not have the luxury of large corporate support. The main sponsors were The Coca-Cola Company and Anheuser-Busch. For this event, we were relying on gate receipts. We had not sold enough tickets and time was running out. This was critical because our commitment at the time to FAMU and Tennessee State was to place $100,000 each year into a quasi-endowment fund.

The money for printing, advertising, and other expenses associated with the game had been obtained through a loan from our Le Cabaret account. At a meeting, the members had agreed to approve this loan and replace the monies immediately after the game.

There was no way we were going to call the game off, so we began to search for solutions to raise more money. We called the athletic directors for FAMU and Tennessee State, Dr. Walter Reed and Bill Thomas, and they assured us that we had their full support to sell even more tickets. However, we still had to guarantee both school $100,000 each.

One of our members, Casdell Singleton, was Vice President of Citizens Trust Bank at the time. He worked with us to secure a line of credit to pay FAMU and Tennessee State University. Even with his support and that of the colleges, our financial problems continued to grow.

In the midst of our dealing with low ticket sales, we received a call from an attorney at Johnson Publishing Company who wanted to talk to us about using the name Atlanta Ebony Football Classic.

James Mac Hunter, Esq.
General Counsel, 100 Black Men of Atlanta, Inc. and 100 Black Men of America, Inc.
By-Laws Committee Member
Partner, Morris, Manning and Martin, LLP

At the time of our first football classic, Ebony Magazine was fifty years old. After conducting some legal research, we discovered that Johnson Publishing had no legal trademark rights in the sporting class to the name, "Ebony." But it was more than a legal matter to both parties so in July 1989, I flew to Chicago with Dr. Joseph Hoffman, Richard Sinkfield, and Leon Oldham to attend a meeting with Mr. John H. Johnson.

You have to respect the fact that as a statesman for black men all over the world, Mr. Johnson had been closely associated with the name "Ebony" for fifty years. It was more than just business to him - it was part of his family legacy.

Mr. Johnson was a good man and he respected the fact that we were a group of black men trying to do the right thing for young people. He was concerned for us and did not want to cause any problems that would create a financial loss for the organization. Instead of a long drawn out legal battle, we shook hands and agreed that 100 Black Men of Atlanta, Inc. would use the name Ebony Classic in 1989 only. The following year Mr. Johnson agreed to publicize our game with its new name to notify the public that the game would continue under a different name.

Dr. Joseph I. Hoffman, Jr.

We had an exciting pep rally the day before the Ebony Classic.   On the day of the game, September 23, 1989, Georgia Tech's Grant Field was filled to capacity with 44,000 people. Another 5,000 were standing outside trying to gain entry. There was no room in the inn, and it was a glorious day.

Thanks to our member's suggestion to host that game, we were able to start our Saturday Academy for the Project Success students.

(Left to right) Atlanta Tribune Publisher, Patricia Lottier accepts an award from President Joseph I. Hoffman, Jr. and President-Elect William "Sonny" Walker, at a reception during the Atlanta Football Classic.

ATLANTA
EBONY CLASSIC I

$3.00

Tennessee State vs Florida A&M   Atlanta/Sept. 23, 1989/2 p.m.
Grant Field at Georgia Tech

Souvenir Program for the 100 Black Men of Atlanta, Inc.'s first football game, originally named Atlanta Ebony Classic.

Monica B. Douglas

Thanks to the success of the game we started our Saturday Academy at Atlanta Metropolitan College. It had two major components: academic and leadership development. The Academy was held every Saturday from 8:30 am to 2:00 pm for a period of fifteen weeks. During this time, the students were tutored in Reading, English, Math, Computer Science, SAT Preparation and Study Skills.

Despite the additional assistance the students were receiving through the Saturday Academy, many of them showed no academic improvement. Some continued to miss their regular classes at Archer High School, and started to miss Academy classes on Saturday.

This situation concerned me deeply. I felt it was time for us to start holding the students more accountable for their grades. I went to the members and suggested that we reinforce the Saturday Academy by having each student and their parents sign another covenant agreement like they had when we started Project Success two years earlier. The members agreed with the hopes that this would reinforce the commitment all of us had made to the students' education.

Even after the students and parents signed the covenant again, some of the students continued to show little or no improvement in their academics. This was disheartening for all of us, and we knew we had to take drastic steps if we wanted to turn the situation around. For the first time ever, we put eleven students on probationary status with the intent to re-evaluate their interest and level of participation in Project Success. One student eventually withdrew from the program after he was placed on probation. His departure sent a strong message to the other students whose grades were not up to standard. They could not remain a part of Project Success if they were not willing to do their part.

Although some students were struggling, many were doing well. That pleased all of us, and we did everything we could to encourage the students' progress.

To help all of the students become well-rounded, we began to expose them to more culturally-related activities. We also believed this would help prepare them for the social life that college would offer. We took them to functions like the "I Dream a World" photo exhibit, which honored 100 black women who had a significant impact on the politics, culture, and arts in this country. The exhibit, which was held at the Woodruff Arts Center, was sponsored by the 100 Black Men of Atlanta and the Metropolitan Atlanta Coalition of 100 Black Women.

Our students really benefited from these outings. They began to see the world differently after being exposed to new environments, new people, and new experiences. They were beginning to participate in some of the exciting and interesting things that can be found in the City of Atlanta. As a result, some of the students began to test their wings and try new things that would've never been available to them before. One student, Alphia Stephens, who was mentored by Terrell L. Slayton, Jr. served as a student Ambassador in England for five weeks.

Alphia Stephens (Chrissy)
Project Success Phase I
Samuel H. Archer Comprehensive High School, Class of 1991
Xaxier University, Class of 1995

My journey to serve as a Student Ambassador in England is one I will never forget. Several students applied for the internship through a series of interviews and a written essay. At the time I was fifteen years old, and I had never dreamed I would travel to England before graduating from high school. But I was chosen, and I couldn't have been happier or more excited.

During my stay in London, I lived with a Greek family who only spoke the Greek language. Therefore, all of my communication with them had to be translated by their daughter. I was a world away from home, but it was exciting to be in a strange land living with this family and learning about their culture and the culture of the City of London. The experience helped me grow as a person and as a student.

I had the support of the 100 while I was in England, and that helped me a great deal. I also had their support when I returned to Atlanta, especially from my mentor, Terrell Slayton. He has always been there for me, cheering me on.

Terrell and the other members of the 100 Black Men of Atlanta also helped me achieve another dream: going to college. All of my life, I wanted to go to college but, because of my family's financial situation, I thought I would have to go to a school in Atlanta or some where else in the State of Georgia. But after I signed up for Project Success, I was able to dream bigger. I graduated from Xavier University in 1995, and received a master's degree from American Intercontinental University in 2000.

When people ask me how the 100 affected me, my first thought is "options." The 100 gave me the option of succeeding or not succeeding. They gave me the option of becoming the person I wanted to become. They gave me the option of going to the college of my choice as long as I maintained a "B" average. I will always be grateful to 100 Black Men of Atlanta for giving me the option to be a better person and to have a better life than I ever dreamed.

January 28, 1991

To: Ms Monica Douglas, Mr John Grant
One Hundred Black Men of Atlanta Inc.
Project Success

My name is Rosemary Stephens. My daughter, Alphia is a member of homeroom 12-1.

I just want to take this moment to say thanks.

Your program has given Alphia opportunities that she probably would not have had.

She has seen things, gone to places and become involved in activities that were only dreams for us.

Being a part of Project Success has motivated Alphia to become more serious about her school work and develope a mature sense of what she wants to do for the next five or six years after high school. And even beyond.

Thanks for the strong "Father" relationships that Alphia has developed with her mentors. Terrell Clayton has helped our family on several occasions when I had no one else to ask. We would not know him if we were not a part of Project Success. Thanks again!

I would also like to thank the One Hundred Black Men for the scholarships that were given to two of my daughters Andreia, Valedictorian, Class of '90 and Alison, Salutatorian Class of '87.

Your organization has given hope to a lot of your people and for the Stephens Family. We will forever be grateful.

Sincerely,
Rosemary Stephens

Terrell L. Slayton, Jr.
Board Member, 100 Black Men of Atlanta, Inc.
Assistant Secretary of State
Office of Secretary of State Cathy Cox

Being Chrissy's mentor helped me to grow as a man and as a human. In many ways, she helped me more than I helped her.

I thought long and hard before I joined the 100 Black Men of Atlanta. I did not want to join another organization for the sake of being able to put their name on my vitae. I wanted to belong to a group that was really committed to helping the community, mainly young people. The 100 Black Men of Atlanta was the answer to my prayers. I was really impressed with the fact that they had adopted an entire class of students at Archer High School.

Almost immediately after joining, I asked for a student to mentor. They assigned me to Chrissy. But she quickly became more than just a mentee, more than someone for me to give advice and guidance. She became another daughter to me, someone whom I have grown to love and cherish for almost twenty years.

Chrissy was always a good student, and that meant the two of us had free time to do things together that were not related to academics. We went to the theatre, the park, and many other places that she had never experienced.

I was there when Chrissy graduated from Archer High School. I was also there with tears in my eyes when she received her undergraduate and graduate degrees.

It has been a pure joy to watch Chrissy grow into the fine young woman that she is today. I will always be there for my Chrissy.

The state of Georgia has an important role in meeting the needs of Georgia's children. However, truly meeting the needs of our young people goes far beyond what government alone can do. No state agency or program is a substitute for loving parents, a nurturing home environment, or a true community of caring individuals that recognize the importance of shaping the next generation. This is one of the most important types of stewardship any of us can undertake. 100 Black Men of Atlanta is a perfect example of these ideals in action.

The Honorable Sonny Perdue
Governor, State of Georgia

Dr. Joseph I. Hoffman, Jr.

There is no crisis greater in an organization than the change of leadership in the middle of an administration. In January 1990, our president-elect, Dr. Charles Meredith was offered the position as President of New York City Technical College in Brooklyn, New York. After accepting his new position, Dr. Meredith gave his official resignation in April, and William "Sonny" Walker became our president-elect following a very close special election between him and Thomas W. Dortch, Jr.

After Sonny's inauguration, our first mission as president and president-elect was to work together to further enhance the success of our football game. Though the first game was a success, it was filled with trials and errors that we wanted to correct before the 1990 game.

One of the main areas that we wanted to improve was pre-publicity. Starting our advertisements early was the first step. Just as he had promised, Mr. John Johnson of Ebony Magazine began advertising the game in the July issues of Jet and Ebony magazines. He even sent a reporter and a photographer to the President's Luncheon and to Le Cabaret to get a first-hand look at these events before the game in September.

Due to the publicity surrounding the organization, we had begun to receive inquiries from African American men outside of Atlanta who wanted to gain more knowledge about our organization and possibly start their own chapters in other metropolitan areas. In June 1990, the 100 Black Men of South Metro was formed in the Riverdale/Clayton County area. A delegation of members from our organization attended the event to show our support for them and their efforts.

The leadership that we had shown through our mentoring program, Project Success, also prompted us to nominate Nate Goldston as a candidate for national president of 100 Black Men of America, Inc. in 1989. The truth is Nate is such a modest man that he really did not want to put his name in the election process, but the members insisted. We knew what an effective leader he was, and we felt he could help guide the national organization as it continued its mission. It turned out that Nate was the only candidate and the elections were rescheduled for June 28th at the 1990 convention in New Jersey. The candidates in 1990 were Nate and New Jersey chapter member, Earl Lofton.

Nathaniel R. Goldston, III

Joe is correct when he says I did not want to run for national president of the 100 Black Men of America, Inc. It was not because I did not want to help further our cause, I am just a strong believer that everybody can and should serve. Because I had already served as president of the 100 Black Men of Atlanta for three years, I was open to someone else having an opportunity to serve on the national level.

I was not present at the convention in New Jersey when I won the election. I was in St. Louis at my family reunion when I received a call from a few members who had gathered in their hotel room to call me with the good news. I will never forget the range of emotions that I felt that night. There was truly a feeling of brotherhood among African American men who are trying to make a difference.

Dr. Joseph I. Hoffman, Jr.

The year 1990 was a defining year for the 100 Black Men of Atlanta for many reasons, but one that we will never forget is the day Nelson Mandela came to Atlanta.

The world stood still when Mr. Mandela was released from Victor Verster Prison on February 11, 1990. Within months of his release, he traveled to Atlanta as part of his United States Tour. Hundreds of thousands of people flocked to our city just to get a glimpse of this great man and to hear his words.

Following Mr. Mandela's speech, the 100 Black Men of Atlanta hosted a reception for him at the Wardlaw Center at Georgia Institute of Technology. We were all honored to welcome him to our country and our State. We were honored to be in his presence and to see the dignity and humanity that had sustained him while he was in prison.

After Mr. Mandela's visit to Atlanta, we began to once again focus our energy on the upcoming football game. Dr. Norman Johnson served as our new chairman. He had a new plan for what was becoming a major event in the city of Atlanta. We were all excited about his vision, and eager to help him put it into action.

Members of the 100 Black Men of Atlanta, Inc. join members of the Atlanta community to welcome Mr. Nelson Mandela to Atlanta, June, 1990.

Dr. Norman J. Johnson
Former Assistant to the President, Georgia Institute of Technology
Professor/Director, FAMU-School of Business and Industry

One of the most exciting things about our second football game was that we gave the Project Success students an opportunity to participate. They worked with the students in both of the college bands and they greeted our sponsors. Our students were very excited to talk to college students for the first time. They asked them about the schools they were attending and about college life in general.

The football game was a huge success. In fact, we filled Grant Field with so many people the fire marshals were called.

Given the success of that day, we had no idea that the annual football classic we were working so hard to solidify in the City of Atlanta was in jeopardy. We were days away from signing our contract for the third game the following year when negotiations broke down between us and the colleges. The main contention was that each college wanted a minimum of $200,000 plus $35,000 to cover the band and travel expenses. Their reasoning was clear. They felt the success of the game was due to the thirty-year-old rivalry between the two teams and their two famous bands, and therefore they should have a greater share of the money that was generated.

In no way did we try to undermine or devalue their position. We were just not in a financial position to meet their demands. The best offer we could make at the time was to split the proceeds three ways, but both colleges rejected our offer. To make matters worse, we discovered that the two colleges were still planning to come to Atlanta and play at the Atlanta Fulton County Stadium on the same day we had planned if we could not come to an agreement.

Unfortunately, we weren't able to come to terms with the colleges. That meant we had to find two new teams to play in our football game. It took some effort but we found them: Southern University and South Carolina State. We scheduled the game for 7:00 p.m. at Georgia Institute of Technology. We braced ourselves for the fact that all four teams would be playing in Atlanta on the same day, but at different times. There was little we could do about this situation, except hope that the fans would have enough energy for two games.

We had worked so hard to continue our football game because we were determined to keep the commitment we had made to our students to pay for their college tuition. In addition to the fact that we had a class graduating in the upcoming year, we were also in heavy discussions about adopting a new group of students from Clara M. Pitts, William M. Boyd, and William J. Scott Elementary Schools. However, we did not intend to make any immediate commitment to pay these students' college tuition.

Members Delmar L. Corbin (left) and Henry A. Kelly (right) emphasize the importance of education to students at William M. Boyd Elementary School.

Joseph I. Hoffman, Jr.

Initially, Phase II was to only serve as a mentoring program. We were not financially prepared at that time to commit to paying for the new students' post-secondary. We needed every dollar we had raised to pay the tuition for our Phase I students, who would begin their first year of college in 1991.

Monica Douglas, John Grant, and the Project Success Committee were all working tirelessly to prepare the Project Success students for college. In the midst of this, we all recognized we could no longer effectively operate our organization and Project Success relying only on the members, as dedicated as they were, and a paid staff of one.

We began to explore the possibility of hiring an office manager without using the money we had allocated for our student's education. While we conducted a citywide search to fill the position, one of our dedicated members, Leonard P. Chambliss, Jr., went to his employer at IBM and asked to be placed on executive loan to the 100 Black Men of Atlanta for one year.

Leonard P. Chambliss, Jr.
Board Member, 100 Black Men of Atlanta, Inc.
President and Owner, Amenity Homes, LLC

I had been an employee at IBM for a number of years when I requested a leave of absence to become the Vice-President of Development for the 100 Black Men of Atlanta. I was familiar with IBM's executive loan program because a number of my associates had participated in the same program to work at colleges and universities across the country.

Within one week of my employment with the 100 Black Men of Atlanta, I began trying to find two new teams for our football game that was less than six months away. One of my best friends, Willie Jeffries, was the head football coach at South Carolina State. I contacted him to see if he was interested. Willie liked the idea and immediately began the process of working out a contract with us while we searched for a second team. Through the efforts of Curley Dossman, Sr., father of member Curley M. Dossman, Jr., who was on the Board of Directors at Southern University, we were able to get Southern University to be the second football team.

After we had secured the two teams for our football classic, they would remain our partners for the next three years, we had to assure the fans that the game would still be great entertainment for the City of Atlanta.

Dr. Joseph I. Hoffman

After we had completed our search for a new office manager, we realized we had received a blessing. It was one of the many blessings this organization has received over the years. Her name is Karen D. Roberts, and she is wonderful. Karen was not new to our organization; she had worked with Dr. Clemons for years at Atlanta Junior College (now Atlanta Metropolitan College) managing the school's reading laboratory. He had also recruited her to serve as a volunteer with the 100 Black Men two years before she became our office manager.

Karen has been loyal beyond words to the students of Project Success and to the 100 Black Men of Atlanta, Inc. None of us know what we would do without her.

Karen D. Roberts
Office Manager, 100 Black Men of Atlanta, Inc.

In 1987, Dr. Willie Clemons asked me to work as a volunteer for the 100 Black Men of Atlanta. Volunteers acted as chaperones, tutors, and event hostesses.

When Dr. Clemons suggested that I apply for the office manager position, I did not hesitate at all. I was already very familiar with the organization and the Project Success Program. I had worked with the students in Saturday Academy on a number of occasions. I was well aware of the 100 Black Men of Atlanta's commitment to the young people in Atlanta, and that reassured me that this was the right position for me.

On March 11, 1991, I moved into the office space at 615 Peachtree Street in downtown Atlanta with Monica and Leonard. The space was small, but we made the best of our new situation.

Just as my new position began, we gained a new president, Sonny Walker.

William 'Sonny' Walker

Former President, 100 Black Men of Atlanta, Inc.
Principal and CEO, The Sonny Walker Group

The most exciting thing that happened during my term as president was when the class we adopted at Archer High School graduated. It was 1991 and my first month in office. I, and all of the members, were extremely proud of our students and what they had accomplished. It is a night I will never forget.

When we adopted that class in 1987, there were two hundred students in the 8th grade class. Five years later, there were only ninety-two graduating seniors. Of those ninety-two students, thirty-one were Project Success students. We had added four students to our original twenty-seven. When Dr. Dixon addressed the graduating class, he asked the students who were going on to post-secondary school to stand. Thirty-five stood.

"My God," I thought when I learned later that thirty-one of them were Project Success students. I cannot speak for other members, but for me that was a defining moment. I became more determined than ever to help as many students as possible receive a quality college education and fulfill their dreams.

Little did the founding members realize how much their initial meeting would impact hundreds of young people's lives.

Karen D. Roberts
Office Manager
100 Black Men of Atlanta, Inc.

Project Success Phase I students 1991.

Antonio Thomas, Project Success Phase I student (third from left) during graduation
ceremony for Archer High School, 1991.

William "Sonny" Walker

Attending Archer's 1991 graduation was also very sobering for me because it meant the Project Success students were another step closer to going to college. They would soon be leaving us and starting their adult lives. Graduation also meant our organization was only four months away from having to pay their college tuition.

The students had made it through the toughest part, surviving five years of high school in an area that had a fifty-per cent (50%) drop out rate. Now, eighty percent of them were planning to go off to colleges as far away as New Orleans, Louisiana and Syracuse, New York. Others were planning to stay in Atlanta to attend school.

As President, I started to review where every dollar the organization had was being spent. I have been a member of many organizations and worked tirelessly during the civil rights movement for the future of our young people. One fact that most people do not know about civil rights leaders is that most of them had little or no salaries. If you wanted something for yourself during the movement, you had to pay for it. If you wanted to socialize, you had to pay for it. Because of my experiences, I knew how important it was to use our dollars wisely.

At one of our meetings, I made a motion that effective immediately we had to pay for all activities that did not benefit Project Success. To do that, we agreed to raise our membership dues, and set aside a certain percentage of that money for our holiday party. My efforts to tighten our financial belt did not make me very popular with some of the members. But I believed then as I do now that whatever money we raise should always go towards our mission to educate our Project Success students. In time, I knew the doubters would realize that too.

Members share a moment at a Holiday Celebration. (Left to right: Carlos James, Renee James, Bobby Olive, Leonard Chambliss, Rhonda Chambliss, Ray Robinson, Patricia and Michael Young.)

William "Sonny" Walker

Eventually, the members got used to my new ideas and we moved on to business that was more important. It did not take the members long to see how much money we were saving: money we could use to pay our students' expenses when they left for college.

Late that summer, parents and mentors left Atlanta to take the students to their respective colleges. Once the students were settled in, the members seemed to have a greater sense of responsibility for them financially. They realized the majority of these kids were going to be there for four years because they had proven over the years that they had the interest, determination, drive, and excitement to succeed in college.

We had little time to drown in our sorrows about the fact that the Atlanta Football Classic, as it was now being called, was about to endure a major change. I believe that if the members of the 100 and the two teams looked back at what happened fifteen years ago, we all would have handled the situation in a different way. I can admit now that there were no winners that day. The City of Atlanta was divided, and so were the football fans that had traveled for hundreds of miles.

While the football committee led the charge to secure the new teams and make football game better, other members continued to focus on the plans for Phase II of Project Success. One of the important lessons we learned from the Phase I students was that we had to start mentoring our next group in an earlier grade. We did the best we could with the Phase I students, but the few who dropped out of the program had issues that we might have helped them had we been involved in their lives at an earlier stage. Conditions like early teenage pregnancies might have been avoided through counseling.

The first program we used to assist our new group of students was an idea that Dr. Alonzo Crim brought to us from the Atlanta Public School System called the "Read to Succeed" Program. "Read to Succeed" was designed to help students develop a good structure to read as much as possible. Members were required to go to different schools every second and fourth Wednesday to read to the students. Many of our members were involved with "Read to Succeed," but one of our founding members, Herman L. Reese, led the charge to make the program a success.

Dr. Herman L. Reese

Starting Phase II of Project Success as a reading program was a great opportunity for the members and the students. It gave us a chance to further understand the importance of being a mentor by sitting down and reading a book to the young people. Some members who had never had a mentee volunteered to read to the students.

For many of the students, their only exposure to books had been in the classroom. Several students told us they did not own a book at home. We acted immediately to change that. We approached Scholastic Books and they generously donated two thousand books for students enrolled in Atlanta Public Schools.

For me as a member, a father, and an educator, this project is one of the most important I have ever undertaken. The greatest gift you can give a child, outside of love, is the gift of reading. Reading is freedom from the environment in which you live. You can dream through the written word.

When I think about the wonderful experience of being involved with "Read to Succeed," and the impact that it had on the students in Project Success II, I can only hope that other organizations will develop similar programs to help further educate our children. The rewards to them and the children would be great.

I often think about the influence "Read to Succeed" and being a member of the 100 has had on me.

My whole experience over the last twenty years has changed my life by simply being in the right place at the right time. I was not invited to the Mansion in 1986 for the meeting of the men who would later form the 100. I was there having dinner with a few friends when I ran into Nate and Joseph. Nate told me why they were there and asked if I would be interested in joining the new group they were forming.

Of the thousands of restaurants in Atlanta, God led me to the Mansion that night. He led me to Nate and the Project Success students. That one moment in time changed my life.

Project Success Phase III student Devin Humphrey and 9th President William J. Stanley, III at Le Cabaret in 2002.

I always stop to wonder where I would be without the 100 Black Men of Atlanta. They have helped me accomplish my goals far beyond my dreams, and I do not know where I would be without them.

Devin Humphrey
Student, Project Success Phase III
Senior, Clark Atlanta University

William "Sonny" Walker

The 100 Black Men of Atlanta, Inc. was growing in numbers, but many members were only active because they were still paying their dues. They were not on any committees, and they were not mentoring any students. Some members only showed up for Le Cabaret and the holiday party. We were at the point that the same members were doing all the work, and they were beginning to feel overwhelmed.

In an attempt to solve this problem, I called a meeting of the board of directors and asked each one of the members of the board of directors to become a liaison between the board and the committee chairmen. I also asked that the board liaisons and chairmen strongly encourage every member to serve on at least one committee. Our new plan was very effective. Members who had been not participating before joined committees and started to show more interest in Project Success.

In addition to getting members more involved in the organization, I was also considering ways to make us more effective in the future. I often met with President Elect Thomas Dortch to talk about the future of the 100. In July 1991, Nicolas Goddy, John Grant, Monica Douglas, and I met with Emmett Carson from the Ford Foundation to discuss the Foundation giving a grant of at least $40,000, but not to exceed $45,000, to the 100 Black Men of Atlanta to be used for strategic planning. The Foundation provided the grant, and the 100 contributed $15,000 for our first Strategic Organization Plan from 1993 to 1997.

We also hired two firms, The Institute for Nonprofit Management and Towers Perrin, in a joint venture to help us determine where we were going and why, and to help us examine what our external and internal challenges would be. When the strategic plan was finished, we had an outline of the goals for the 100 Black Men of Atlanta and our students for the next four years.

As I prepared to turn the reins over to Tommy, I began to advocate that we should try to get qualified members of the organization elected to boards throughout our communities in the City of Atlanta. By broadening our base of influence, we would be better able to help our youth through better education and jobs, and we would be able to show them what we could accomplish if we applied ourselves.

I also felt the 100 Black Men of Atlanta should have an impact on the present and the future of our community and the City. I wanted us to sit at the table with our influential leaders and talk about the preservation of the history of Atlanta. For example, the Butler Street YMCA that is located two blocks from our current office has a strong history in this community. Leaders like Maynard Jackson, Vernon Jordan, and many other black men who helped shape America once played at that YMCA.

It is our responsibility to tell our children where our leaders' lives started. We have to hold on to our heritage not just for the children in Project Success, but also for the history of this nation.

I remember going back to my hometown of Pine Bluff, Arkansas to take my grandchildren to see the gymnasium where I played basketball in high school. I wanted them to see where I got my education and all the trophies we had won as a team. When we drove up, the school was no longer there. In its place was a warehouse. My grandchildren looked at me real strange and said, "Grandpa you went to high school in a warehouse?"

If people can preserve the Margaret Mitchell House, we as the 100 Black Men of Atlanta can help preserve Paschal's Restaurant and the YMCA. I'm not anti-white. I'm just pro-black. I think we need to understand our own history to be able to teach our children.

The 100 can be a part of the preservation process. We cannot have permanent friends or permanent enemies in the political arena. We must have permanent representation for the interest in the future of our young people. We must have interest in closing the academic gap between our children and all races. Our mayor, Shirley Franklin, said it best when she was laying a wreath at Maynard Jackson's gravesite, "We cannot just go around laying wreaths to honor men and women. We must honor the principles that they stood for." Long after the Republicans and Democrats are gone, we have the principles of mankind to fall back on. Let that be a part of the legacy of this great organization.

Thomas W. Dortch, Jr.
Past President, 100 Black Men of Atlanta, Inc.
Past Chairman, 100 Black Men of America, Inc.
President and CEO, TWD, Inc.

The first time I campaigned for president-elect of 100 Black Men of Atlanta, I lost the election to my good friend and mentor, Sonny Walker. That loss turned out to be a victory for me, because Sonny and I became partners and better friends. I learned so much from Sonny and his style of good leadership.

My relationship with Sonny began long before we were president and president-elect of 100 Black Men of Atlanta. We joined the organization together in 1987, and we served on various committees together.

The first committee I volunteered for was the hospitality committee. This was after the Atlanta chapter had been selected to host the 1987 National Convention.

The 1987 convention set the standard for how the City of Atlanta perceived the 100 Black Men of Atlanta and how other chapters viewed us. The success of the convention and our first Le Cabaret no doubt helped me to understand that we had a special organization that was going to make a difference in the lives of young people.

When I began serving my term as president, I didn't change many of the committee chairs or the way Sonny handled most of the business for this organization. My goal was to finish the job that Sonny and I pledged to do as president and president-elect. Oftentimes when a new president is elected, he or she comes in the door with the intent to reshape the entire organization. I was Sonny's co-pilot for two years and I knew the direction we were traveling together was the right course. Sonny left the 100 Black Men of Atlanta with something that no other president had before, a strategic plan.

In addition to Sonny's strategic plan it was my goal to find economic capacities to diversify the program we already had in place. In order to do that, Sonny and I had already begun to request larger donations from our corporate sponsors and to ask our members to research other fundraising ventures to help fund our Project Success program.

Terrell Slayton suggested that we create an annual golf classic. We would invite corporations to not only sponsor the event, but also to participate in the game. Our first classic was held April 13, 1992 at the Atlanta Athletic Club. Similar to our first football game, the golf classic was very much a learning experience, but we were able to make a profit for the Project Success students.

Because we now had three major events and over thirty students in college at the time, people began to call the office almost daily to get more information about the organization and the programs we offered. In order to raise our public awareness, and to keep our members informed, before leaving office Sonny and I thought it was time we created a newsletter and an annual report that would keep not just our members informed, but the community and our sponsors. To date, both publications are mailed to members, board members, parents, corporate sponsors, and friends of the 100 Black Men of Atlanta.

The response to both publications has always been good. We often received congratulatory notes and calls from those who receive them. We have also noticed that our members have fewer questions at the meeting because they have already read their newsletters and know what is going on within the organization.

Because of our newsletters, annual reports, and positive publicity we received a welcomed call in 1994 from The National Mentoring Partnership. They wanted to talk to us about a new program they were piloting called the Pathways Initiative.

Archibald B. Hill, III
Former Chair, Project Success
100 Black Men of Atlanta, Inc.
Director, Atlanta Partnership-Fannie Mae

The Pathways Initiative was a great opportunity for the Phase II Project Success students. They were excited about it and so were their parents.

Funded largely by The Robert Wood Johnson Foundation, Pathways was designed to provide disadvantaged students who were already in mentoring programs with intensive mentoring and to expose them to different career opportunities over a number of years. One of the National Mentoring Partnership's requirements for eligibility was that each organization had to assign a member to serve as the program manager. I became the program manager for Pathways, and I served as a liaison between our organization and the Partnership. I also worked directly with the students in Pathways.

In addition to the mentoring Project Success students were already receiving from the 100 Black Men of Atlanta, the Pathways Initiative provided personal and economic mentoring, life skills training, entrepreneurial training, and financial incentives. The National Mentoring Partnership set aside $10,000 for twenty of our Project Success students in a managed investment fund. From grades four through twelve, the students received stipends of $50 each quarter from the interest earned on their $10,000. The remaining interest was credited to the students' personal account as undistributed interest. As long as the students met the requirements set by the National Mentoring Partnership from grades four through twelve, after high school graduation, they could take any accumulated interest, along with the $10,000 principal, and use it towards college, technical education, purchasing a house, or starting a business.

The National Mentoring Partnership's requirements for the students were similar to those the 100 Black Men of Atlanta already had in place. All of the students had to maintain an active relationship with a mentor, do well in school, and behave well outside of the classroom.

Although we lost a few Pathways students along the way, many were successful. Star Lowe, who is a senior at Clark Atlanta University, stayed on course and she is now working on a business plan for the company she intends to start after graduating in spring, 2006. Star and her mother had the wisdom to not withdraw her $10,000 after high school graduation. Instead, they left it in the interest bearing account to be withdrawn after she graduates.

Star R. Lowe

Project Success Phases II & III
Senior, Clark Atlanta University

I was so young when I became a part of Project Success. I was too young to understand that being chosen to be a part of this program would change my life forever.

My mother welcomed the help that Project Success provided for my education and me. Because my mother struggles with multiple sclerosis, she has never had the opportunity to truly do the things she planned for my two siblings and herself.

In addition to the Saturday Academy, tutoring during the week, field trips, and the many other things that the 100 had already given me, I was chosen as one of the Pathways students. The twenty students in the 100's Pathways Program received many opportunities from The National Mentoring Partnership. We had the chance to go on additional field trips and meet people in corporate America who talked to us about owning our own companies one day.

Sixteen years later as I prepare for graduation, I have decided to start my own publishing company. Several people have told me that publishing is a difficult business, but life is difficult. When I spoke to author Shelia P. Moses, she told me to follow my dreams. She said, "If you want to be a doctor, don't go to law school." I am going to follow her advice and my dreams.

I am grateful to the Pathways Program for giving me a leg to stand on as I prepare to become a small business owner. I am grateful to the 100 Black Men of Atlanta for just giving me a chance.

Members Archibald B. Hill, III, Westley H. Workman and John S. Hix, spend time with the Project Success students.

Thomas W. Dortch, Jr.

The Pathways Program was just one of the wonderful elements of Project Success. So was the response that we received from other organizations and companies who wanted to help our students.

But our students weren't the only ones who needed help. Our staff also needed assistance.

The organization had simply outgrown the three people who worked for us, and we could no longer expect members to meet the high demands of our day-to-day operations. Therefore, in 1993, we started a nationwide search for our first executive director. Renda Johnson was hired to fill the position. We also hired Tara Rice to serve as staff support for special events and programs.

As much as we gained by adding two new staff members, we felt we had lost four people when Monica Douglas resigned to join The Atlanta Project as their Coordinator for Children and Youth Services. Monica had done a stellar job for us, and we dreaded losing her. Monica's resignation was not an easy transition for the organization, because she had been with us longer than most of the members.

Monica B. Douglas

I do not believe I could have left my position as Programs Director for the 100 Black Men of Atlanta before 1994. Working with those young people was like having children that did not live with me. So much of my job responsibility had taken on a personal meaning. I cared about all of the students, and I just wanted to know that they were going to be alright. However, once the students were either in college or working, I felt I could move on. My children were all grown up.

Years before the students graduated from high school and left for college, I knew that Project Success was effective. The moment of truth for me came when I began to have students who were not in the program stop by my office to ask if they could join Project Success. It was hard to tell them there was no room in the inn. The students that we had room for started on course and most of them are doing well in life. I am just happy that I was a part of shaping their life experience.

Thomas W. Dortch, Jr.

Months passed before we filled Monica's position by hiring Folami Prescott. Folami was excited about her new role at the 100, and she certainly had all of the necessary qualifications to do the job. Her greatest strength was the same as Monica's: she genuinely cared about the students. She also gave more of her time than we could ever compensate her for monetarily.

It is important to understand that our mentoring program is more significant than anything else the organization does. When I became the national president of the 100 Black Men of America, it was very clear to me that I would continue to find a way to provide that type of service to children. As the national president, one of the first plans I implemented under my watch was, "Four for the Future." This program required all the chapters of 100 Black Men to have a mentoring program under one or more of the following four categories: education, mentoring, economic development, and health and wellness.

Each chapter has a different name for their program. For example, 100 Black Men of Charlotte's program is called Movement of Youth. No matter what the name, they all have the same common goal - to educate our youth. We now call the program, "Mentoring the 100 Way."

I knew the importance of a mentoring program from my experiences with 100 Black Men of Atlanta, and wanted to see it replicated. Make no mistake that Project Success set the tone for the other chapters throughout the nation. I wanted 100 Black Men of America to know what we knew. I went in sending the same message, "If you give a child love, support and encouragement, they can compete with any child no matter what their economic background."

For the chapters that do not have the insight to start a mentoring program, the national chapter gives them the support that they need. All of the chapters are required to go through a training program, and mentors are certified after they complete the program.

Dr. Joshua Murfree, who is a trained psychologist, conducts the training all over the country. Additionally, we go outside of our national organization to share the success of our mentoring program. We have conducted workshops for the Boys and Girls Clubs, and worked with Dr. Dorothy I. Height, President of the National Council of Negro Women, to show other organizations the effect that mentoring the right way can have on a child.

Many members have asked why the mentoring training is needed. It's quite simple - all members are not aware of the needs of our youth. A child living in a stable home environment needs a different support system than a child living in a home where there may be abuse or poverty. We had to teach many members that buying gifts for a child and taking him or her to a basketball game is not mentoring.

Mentors have to understand that many of these young people have been let down so often that we are not about to make promises and not keep them. We will finish the job with each one of them if they keep their part of the deal.

Oftentimes, we have had to talk to the student and their mentor about the student's relationship with his or her family. Not all the mentees are from single-family homes. In those cases, it is important for the mentor to respect the father's role in his child's life. Most of them are working two jobs and may be gone all day and sometimes work out of town, but that does not mean the man is not a good father. In those cases, the 100 Black Men apply the "it takes a village" approach.

One of the greatest lessons this organization has learned is the real meaning of a broken home. A broken home is not a home that consists of one parent. A broken home is a home without love. We learned that some of the children in our program have never heard the words "I love you" from their parent's mouth.

We do not go to a school looking for the children with absent fathers. We go looking for the students who need additional love or support. As an organization that plays a vital part in the community of Atlanta, we have to try to look at every situation individually and try to help where help is needed.

Go back seventy-five years to the Depression. The welfare system said to a mother with five hungry children, "You cannot receive a check with a man, even if he is your husband, staying in this house." The system did not care if the father was working or laid off, he had to leave. Unemployed men were leaving home so their wives could get a welfare check.

What the 100 Black Men of Atlanta said when they formed Project Success is we will not rely on the government to educate and assist our children. That is what the 100 Black Men of America teaches the members in its mentoring program. We want our young people to know that we are here now, and we plan to make their lives better.

That is the kind of community I came from and most people over forty know what I am talking about. We grew up a part of a village with people on every block who were not afraid to discipline us when we got out of line. If you misbehaved in school you were taken care of at school, and you knew what "taken care of" meant in the good old days. When you got home, you were "taken care of" again. Teachers, parents, principals, and neighbors all worked together to make us better young people. That formula still works if the community comes back together and understand the lessons of the village.

Leaving office as president of 100 Black Men of America, I will return to the 100 Black Men of Atlanta, and continue to help in the village. And when this is all said and done and this life of mine is over, I just hope that I die empty. Dr. Myles Munroe, who is one of the great religious leaders in the Bahamas, taught me that concept. He said that the most valuable property on earth is in the graveyards. He believes that too many of us take too many things that we can share with others to our graves. I don't plan to do that. I want to share as much as I can with young people. Dr. Monroe also said that too many people have sight with no vision. We see things we can change and never do.

That is what the 100 Black Men of Atlanta and the 100 Black Men of America continue to do - share their vision. As the 100 Black Men of Atlanta were in the process of completing this book, I ended my tenure as the president of the 100 Black Men of America. I never gave up my membership in the Atlanta chapter. It's good to be home.

The academic success of Atlanta Public Schools' students depends on more than school buildings, classrooms and books. Partnerships with organizations in the greater community, like the one we share with 100 Black Men of Atlanta, have a tremendous impact on helping students reach their greatest potential. I expect these same young people will reach back and mentor the generations of those who will follow them.

Beverly L. Hall, Ed.D.
Superintendent of Atlanta Public Schools

Curley M. Dossman, Jr.

In 1989, I became a proud member of the 100 Black Men of Atlanta. I served as treasurer under Dr. Joseph Hoffman's administration. I joined the organization because I was amazed that a small group of men had committed to mentoring not one or two students, but thirty-three students. In addition to their mentoring program, these men committed to paying the students' college tuition.

When I heard the story of how the students were selected, I knew the men of the 100 Black Men of Atlanta were a unique organization. They were going to have a huge impact on the lives of young people.

I was particularly impressed that the 100 Black Men of Atlanta did not go to Archer High School and ask Dr. Dixon for his best students. They went with open hearts and a teacher's name drawn from a hat. This convinced me that they were sincere and committed. They simply knew they wanted to help a group of young people better their lives.

I wanted to fellowship with this group of men who cared so much about someone other than themselves and their own families. Men who wanted to reach out to students who might not have a fair opportunity in life. I am sure the students' parents were doing the best they could, but some of them were simply deprived of many things they needed to excel in life. I, and the men of the 100, wanted to step in and help them fill the gap.

One of the original members of the organization told me that some of the students in Phase I had never been to downtown Atlanta. I could almost understand that if they lived out in Norcross or Lithonia, but you have to keep in mind, Perry Homes was only one mile from downtown.

The 100 Black Men of Atlanta said to them, "You can leave Perry Homes and go downtown. You can go to New York and you can go to London." It was amazing the effect that idea had on the students.

All of the members of the 100 are successful in their own right, and they didn't need to add anything else to their résumés. They were willing to use their successes to benefit the future of young people who may not have had the same opportunities.

After I had served as treasurer for two years, I really started to understand the effect we were having on the students. I knew I would one day seek office as president. When I became president in May 1995, some of the students from Phase I were still enrolled in college or technical schools. But we were not clear on how well they were doing academically, or if they would even graduate.

We asked John Grant to do an academic assessment of each student. John's findings showed that some of the students were not making good grades and some were actually on probation. Folami Prescott also informed us that the students were not staying in touch with their mentors and some were not in touch with their parents. John and Folami suggested that we solicit the help of a person with experience to track the students' progress and visit the colleges to serve as and become a liaison between the students and the members. We were fortunate enough to find Walter Jacobs to do this job for us. He has being instrumental in turning around the lives of so many of the students.

Mr. Walter R. Jacobs, Jr.
H.E.L.P., Inc.
Higher Education and Leadership Preparation

The Phase I students of Project Success were sophomores in colleges when the 100 Black Men of Atlanta asked me to work as a Programs Consultant. The members were very concerned about the number of students who had already dropped out and the number of students who were failing.

I have spent half of my life educating young people. I know from experience that the first step was to let them know that the people back in Atlanta cared about them. Therefore, I told the 100 Black Men that I wanted to visit each of the students.

My journey with them was no different than any other student who was in trouble academically. Some of them were still adjusting to being away from home. The students did not understand that instructors in college don't hold your hand the way high school teachers do.

When I met with the students, I explained to them the importance of working independently of the structure of a teacher and a classroom. I also talked about the importance of completing every task they were assigned.

I soon realized that some of the student's problems stemmed from their needing a tutor. We helped them get the support they needed, and within a few months, they were doing better. I continued to work with them until the last student graduated from college.

In 2003, Ray Singer asked me to come back to work with the Phase III students, who were now seniors in high school. He had come across one of my SAT Assistance Programs the first week he started the job, and he felt I could help him by working as a consultant. I was happy to work with the students again.

I have attended the graduations of over 100 Project Success students. Each time, I have felt like I was watching my own child walk across the stage.

The 100 Black Men of Atlanta reminds us of our potential impact, power and responsibility.

Kenny Leon,
Actor, Director

Curley M. Dossman, Jr.

Mr. Jacobs focused on our Phase I college students, while Folami and the Programs Committee continued to track Phase II students progress. This was helpful because the organization was in the process of making the final decision about changing Phase II into Phase III program.

Because I had served as treasurer, I knew going into my presidency that we did not have enough money to pay the Phase II students' tuition after graduation. We had exactly $360,000 in reserve, and that was needed to pay our Phase I students' tuition. I felt it was time for us to start an endowment fund that would secure enough funds to pay the tuition for the Phase II students, if we made that commitment to them.

We set a goal for a $2 million endowment, including interest, that would cover the cost for the students during middle school, high school, and college through the year 2006. We challenged the community to match the first $1 million raised by the 100. Our co-chair was Tommy Hill from Wachovia Bank, and he was instrumental in helping us to reach out to corporate America to reach our goal.

Our method for raising the money was very simple. We relied upon the success of the Phase I students. When we went into the community, we had more than words to convince people to contribute to our cause. We had documents showing what the students from Archer High School had achieved because we had mentored them in school and helped them go to college.

We could stand proud and tell the president of any corporation in America that two of our students were graduating that year with honors: Alphia Stephens from Xavier University and Sonya Jelks from Syracuse University.

We worked hard to raise the money for the endowment. We knew the money would allow us to help other young people walk across the stage of opportunity.

Today, we still have in excess of one million dollars in the endowment fund.

When Raymond J. McClendon became president, he began the process to officially transform Phase II into our Phase III program as a post-secondary preparation and tuition assistance program. The recruitment and selection began with students we were already mentoring under our Phase II program.

They were doing well at West Fulton Middle School participating in the "Read to Succeed," which was now a weekly after-school program that was now headed by Richard E. Moore.

In addition to our members participating in the mentoring program, we had students from the Shaping A Vision through Empowerment (SAVE), founded by Ms. Corliss Heath, reading and tutoring our students. The SAVE students were enrolled at Clark Atlanta University, Emory, Georgia Tech, Spelman, and other metro Atlanta colleges and universities. The SAVE students also offered workshops on topics such as self-awareness, conflict resolution, goal setting, and male/female responsibility.

We also got help from the Collegiate 100, which was chaired by Dr. William Lynn

We also received help from the Collegiate 100, which was chaired by Dr. William Lynn Weaver. Collegiate 100 began when some of the members of the 100 Black Men of Atlanta started to express their concerns that we were getting older, and therefore the generation gap was widening between us and the students.

Cevin Smithers, a 2000 graduate of Clark Atlanta University, was elected the first President of the Collegiate 100 of Atlanta. Today, he is a Principal Financial Analyst at The Coca-Cola Company. Cevin remains in close contact with the 100 Black Men of Atlanta and the students of Project Success.

Otis Threatt also became a member of the Collegiate 100 while attending Clark Atlanta University and he has been an employee at the 100 Black Men of Atlanta for the past five years.

Otis Threatt, Jr.

Accounting, IT and Events Assistant

I was still a student at Clark Atlanta University when I became affiliated with the 100 Black Men of Atlanta. I joined the Collegiate 100 because I wanted to help other students who wanted to attend college one day. I worked every Saturday with the Project Success Phase III students at the Saturday Academy, which was held at Georgia State University.

Becoming a Collegiate 100 member was a new and exciting experience for me. After I graduated from college, I accepted a part-time position at the 100 BMOA. My degree in Business Administration was supposed to lead me in a totally different direction in corporate America. But I know that God had a different plan for me because when a full-time position with the 100 came available, I took it, and I know it was the right decision for me. Every day when I walk into my office, I know that something new and exciting will happen.

Working for the 100 is not the same as working for corporate America. It is better… I know that every day I am making a difference in a child's life.

Curley M. Dossman, Jr.

Having the Collegiate 100 of Atlanta work with us was a big help because we needed these young people to help us relate better to our students. They were close in age, and therefore they understood what the Project Success students were thinking and feeling. The Collegiate 100 also assisted Archibald Hill with field trips for the Pathways students, who were really thriving. They traveled with twenty Pathway students when they went to Babson College in Massachusetts for a one-week entrepreneurship program. The trip was sponsored by Carson Products.

The Collegiate 100 also assisted our organization in administering components for Phase III of Project Success. After filling twenty slots for the program with Pathways students, we had a difficult selection process for eighty additional students. People in the community wanted help for their children and we had more applicants than available space. When the process was complete, we had 118 students in the program.

But we would soon face a more serious issue - a new group of students with no program director aboard. Folami Prescott resigned from her position to embark on new endeavors. Folami left Project Success in a good place. She really cared about the students and that showed in her work. Before she left, she arranged for the students to recommit themselves to Project Success by signing a new covenant on March 2, 1998.

Keldrin R. Blount
Project Success, Phase II and III
Sophmore, Hampton University

I remember like it was yesterday when we were told that we were going to receive college tuition just like the students in Phase I. The parts that I didn't understand, my mother explained to me. She told me that I had the opportunity of a lifetime to go to college. She laid down the new rules of what I had to do to stay in Project Success. Although I was very young at the time, I understood what my mother was saying and I wanted to try.

I had been in Phase II from its inception. From that first day sixteen years ago, my life has never been the same again. That's because of my mentor, Albert Kemp, Jr., who has been at my side to help and guide me in any way he could. He has been the father I never had. Everything I know about being a man, I learned from Mr. Kemp. He taught me how to survive outside of the environment that I lived in.

I have gained so much from being a Project Success student, but I will always treasure that I gained a father in Mr. Kemp and a best friend for life, Erica McGinty. Erica McGinty lived in the same neighborhood with me, and we both were chosen for Project Success. Because we did not know the other students, we stayed close to each other at the functions. We went from elementary school to middle school together. When it was time to go to high school, we only separated during school hours because Erica attended Douglass High and I attended Northside High School. Mr. Kemp suggested I enroll at Nothside High because I was interested in the arts. Every day after school, Erica and I did our homework together, and we talked about our lives and going to college. When it was time to go away to college, we both chose Hampton University in Virginia. Hampton had what we both wanted academically, and it allowed us to stay together. We have become like sister and brother.

Just think - out of Project Success, I have gained a father, hundreds of men who care about me, a full scholarship to college, and a best friend for life.

Project Success students, Keldrin Blount and Erica McGinty celebrate with 100 member John S. Hix, Jr. after receiving their stipends for the completion of the Ben Carson Summer Science Academy, 1998.

Gwen Julien
Finance Manager
100 Black Men of Atlanta, Inc.

I watched Keldrin and Erika grow as students and as young people, just as I watched the 100 Black Men of Atlanta, Inc. grow into the fine organization that it has become. I joined the staff during Ray McClendon's administration as the first finance manager.

I was amazed at the assistance the 100 provided to the students and their education. As a single mother, I know firsthand that it takes a lot of money to send a child to college. So I appreciate so much what the 100 Black Men of Atlanta have done for the children in Project Success.

I appreciated them even more when I think about my own son David who was affected deeply by the serious financial problems at Morris Brown College. Before the school closed, he was a happy college student with financial aid to cover his tuition. Overnight, he was out of school and back at home with a $20,000 tuition bill to pay.

I pray for my son every day and I do hope the opportunity to go back to school will come for him. I hope that all young people have the opportunity for higher education.

*A twenty year investment is a small amount of time
to invest into the lives of young people.*

Charles Kelley
Board of Directors, 100 Black Men of Atlanta, Inc.
Vice President - Sales
ProGraphics Communications, Inc.

Curley M. Dossman, Jr.

There are so many students with situations similar to Gwen's son David. When a Project Success student is faced with financial problems related to their tuition, the 100 believes it our duty to solve the problem to the best of our ability.

Gwen and other staff members work hard to make our students lives better each day. No amount of money we raise can give them love. In 1998, the 100 hired Kenya N. Summerour as our Senior Programs Associate, who is another example of going the extra mile to help our students every day.

Kenya N. Summerour
Senior Programs Associate
100 Black Men of Atlanta, Inc.

I started my employment here in April 1998, and I have watched the organization go through many changes. I have watched the students grow up to be fine young men and women. When I started, the students had just signed their covenant to become a part of what we now call Project Success Phase III. Although the students were still young, they understood the program had changed and they were required to do more. New requirements were in place such as attending the Ben Carson Science Academy at Morehouse College each weekday during the summer from 8:30 a.m. until 4:00 p.m.

Dr. Vernon L. Allwood
Morehouse School of Medicine
Assistant Professor

In 1994, the Morehouse School of Medicine received a grant from the Howard Hughes Medical Institute to develop a series of programs to help disadvantaged students pursue careers in medicine and biomedical science. When I was contacted by the Institute, they told me that they wanted the program to be named after a positive role model in medicine. I contacted Dr. Benjamin Carson, who said yes when I asked permission to use his name.

This program was ideal for Project Success, and we became partners in 1998, after the Phase III students signed their covenants. Our agreement to enroll Project Success students was a perfect match. Each summer, the students come to Morehouse for six weeks and experience every opportunity we can provide to help them become scientist one day. The elementary and middle school students who attend this program have the opportunity to enhance their knowledge of science, mathematics, and health careers. They also participate in field trips, cultural activities, such as chess, African Dance, Brazilian martial arts, gymnastics and Kiswahili. Over the years, the program has expanded to include both a six- week Summer Science Camp and a Saturday Academy.

As we celebrate our tenth anniversary, I am proud to say that we have enrolled 1,289 since the inception of the Ben Carson Science Academy.

Kenya Summerour

It is my responsibility to make sure that our students are receiving the basics they need to prepare themselves for high school and college. They need so much to prepare them for the competitive academic world. In recent years, colleges have begun to require computers as a fundamental component of their curriculum. The 100 has worked with companies such as IBM and The Coca-Cola Company to help secure laptops for our students upon their graduating from high school. In 2004, two of our members, T. Wayne Kauffman and Francis M. Edward, were able to get IBM, their employer, to give us fourteen laptops, which we gave to students on an as-needed basis.

So much is given to the students, but love is always the most important gift of all. I am not much older than some of the students in the program, and I really try to relate to them and to understand what they have to deal with every day. But I try not to be too easy on them, because I want them to know how fortunate they are. I want them to know that I did not have anyone to buy my books or pay my tuition when I was in college, and that most people don't have that luxury.

I am thankful for my own good fortune for being in this position. I graduated from Tuskegee University in 1993, with a business degree and I received my master's degree from Clark Atlanta University in 1996. I did not plan to stay with the 100 Black Men for all these years, but this job has become a great part of my life. I am so attached to the students and their parents. I honestly feel that this is my purpose in life, to serve others.

Project Success Phase III students pose with 100 staff members at the President's Dinner on April 22, 2004 at the Grand Hyatt Atlanta Hotel, Atlanta, Georgia.

Curley M. Dossman, Jr.

Kenya is one of the thousands of blessings the 100 Black Men of Atlanta has received since starting Project Success. She has been a second mother to some of the students. She believes in the students, and they trust her.

Like Dr. Crim, I believe that every child can learn. I believe that our organization has tried to help our students better their education and to be better men and women. We've also worked to make them good examples for others in our community.

We cannot let America believe that black men don't take care of their children. I pray we will continue to be able to serve the Project Success students and, in turn, they will make the world better for the generation after them.

Bernard M. Porché

After Ray's term as president, we were blessed to have James W. (Jim) George elected as our new leader. Unfortunately, James' term was for only a short while. Jim died too young, too soon. He loved life, his family, and the 100 Black Men of Atlanta.

After Jim became president and I president-elect, Jim and I spent five hours at his house one Saturday planning for the next four years. He had many good ideas about how the 100 could grow, and could continue improving its mentoring programs.

At that time, I did not know how sick he was and that we would have only six months to work together.

During his brief term as president, Jim worked tirelessly to fulfill his commitment to this organization.

He cared deeply about the Project Success students, and he was always trying to encourage our members to spend more time with the students, even if we were not their mentors.

In May 1999, Jim arranged a Job Shadow Day between the members and the students. Members were asked to select a student to spend the day with them at their place of employment. The members picked the students up from their schools early that morning. They spent the rest of the day with the member watching him carry out his duties. We wanted the students to get a real-life experience of what it means to go to work everyday.

This type of program excited Jim because he believed there was no better way to spend our time than with the students.

Though Jim George's term was a brief one, he clearly had a plan as to how the organization should move forward into the new millennium.

Steven W. Smith
Vice President Corporate Affairs
Turner Broadcasting System, Inc.
Member, 100 Black Men of Atlanta, Inc.

William J. Stanley, III, FAIA, NOMA
Past President, 100 Black of Atlanta, Inc.
Principal, Stanley, Love-Stanley, P.C.

Jimmy and I grew up together. I remember his uncle ran a day camp here in Atlanta, and I participated every year. Like his family, Jim always had a sense of obligation to the community.

As president, Jim was very concerned about how we related to each other as men, not just as members. He would invite members to his house just to talk when he had free time. He would preach to us about the Willie Lynch story. He asked each one of us to read this document so that we would learn about the impact that slavery had on African Americans.

Jim also wanted us to understand and stop the cycle of violence in our own communities. He wanted us to be a good example of brotherly love.

If Jim were alive today, he would still be teaching and preaching to us about how to treat one another. He would still have cookouts just to get us together to be kind to each other.

Bernard M. Porché

Losing Jim tested the 100 Black Men of Atlanta just like death will test any family. We were all very sad and hurt, but the loss also pulled us together. It made us appreciate each other more. It made us appreciate our organization more.

Jim came to the 1999 Atlanta Football Classic in a wheelchair. We all thought he was doing better after having recently undergone surgery to have his leg removed. Unfortunately, that was not the case. A few weeks later on October 12, 1999, Jim presided over his last meeting. He was in great spirits and conducted the meeting like he had always done, with brotherly love.

Jim died a short time later. We will never forget his contributions to the 100 Black Men of Atlanta. We believe it is our responsibility to continue to build upon all the things he taught us.

Richard H. Byrd
Past Chaplain, 100 Black Men of Atlanta, Inc.
Public Health Advisor, U.S. Department of Health and Human Services

At the meeting on October 12, 1999, none of us knew Jim's time with us was almost over, but I will always believe he knew he would never see some of us again. I deeply regret that we did not realize how short our time together would be. But Jim was not sad or depressed. He had worked to do, and he expected us to do it.

During the meeting, Jim asked me to create a five-member committee to provide spiritual guidance to members during a time of crisis such as death or illness. It was just like Jim to want to do something to help others. When he died, the article in the newspaper referred to his love of life and his desire to help people around him. For example, Jim, a twenty-eight year employee at Georgia Power, often sent roses to the wives of employees whose husbands were out working for days during power outages. Everybody knew this about him, and I'm sure they loved and respected him for it. Jim did not care about positions, he cared about people.

Our beloved 7th president James W. George (center) sharing a laugh with Bernard and Bobbie Porché.

Bernard M. Porché

It was hard to step in and try to comfort our members and staff who loved Jim so much. Losing Jim was the first time the organization had faced death among us, and it was difficult. We all needed time to grieve.

My goal as the new president was to complete the mission that Jim and I had agreed to that day we met in his home. We had a four-year plan, not a two-year plan, so I picked up the torch from that point and went forward.

At the organization's first meeting on November 3, 1999, after Jim's death, Joe Hoffman made a motion and it was seconded by Eugene Merriday that I would assume and carry out the responsibilities and duties of the president. However, I would not be officially sworn in until April 2000, my original date to be inaugurated. It was also decided that we would not hold an election for president-elect. We voted to have our former president, Ray McClendon, serve as my advisor until April 2000, when William J. Stanley would take office as president-elect. We did not change our cabinet members. The executive board remained in place, and we were able to finish what we had started under Jim's leadership.

One of Jim's missions was to take the Atlanta Football Classic to another level financially. The last game had not provided the revenue that we had predicted. That was primarily because it was scheduled for the same week as the Congressional Black Caucus, and many people were in Washington, D.C. attending that conference.

Before Jim died, the two of us had discussed approaching Georgia Power about becoming our title sponsor. After Jim's death, Georgia Power agreed, and became our first title sponsor largely because they wanted to honor Jim, and they believed in Project Success.

After addressing other issues related to the football game, I started to work on other agenda items. I wrote a letter to the president of the Atlanta Chamber of Commerce. I acknowledged that the Chamber is about business development, but there is no reason that one of the leading nonprofit organizations in the City should not have representation on the Chamber. I was appointed to the Chamber's advisory board representing the 100. I also provided information about our football game to the Atlanta Sports Council, which is part of the Chamber. They were surprised to learn the Atlanta Football Classic rivaled the Peach Bowl. They arranged to have impact studies done. It showed that the economic impact of our classic was substantial for Atlanta. These results confirmed we were not only making a difference in the lives of our students, but we were also affecting the economic growth of the City.

We knew before the impact study that we were making a difference. We knew we were changing the lives of the Project Success students. We were also impacting the lives of the students' parents and their siblings.

Many parents in the program understand the value of Project Success to their child, and to their entire home. They do everything they can to take full advantage of programs we offer their children. Estella McGinty, mother of my second mentee Erica McGinty, is an example of a parent who saw the good in the 100, and the benefits we could provide her daughter. She is the mother you know will always be there, not just for Erica, but for all the other Project Success students as well.

Estella McGinty
Project Success Phase III, Parent

My daughter, Erica, has been a part of Project Success Phase III since she was in the 4th grade. As a single mother, I welcomed the opportunity to let a group of fine men like the 100 Black Men of Atlanta help my daughter.

Erica's relationship with the Porchés has been a positive one, filled with love and respect for my daughter and her well-being. They have not only welcomed her into their family, they have made me a part of their lives as well. I look forward to exchanging gifts with them at Christmas and on our respective birthdays. It is a show of gratitude to each other to give and receive tokens of love.

We all have the same common goal - we want what is best for Erica. The 100 Black Men of Atlanta wants what is best for all of their students.

The 100 Black Men of Atlanta are leading our youth and our community to embrace the impossible.

Gloria S. Elllison
Event Coordinator, 100 Black Men of Atlanta, Inc.

Bernard M. Porché

Even with the help of great parents like Estella, dedicated members, generous sponsors, and an exceptional staff, we were still missing a key element for the 100 Black Men of Atlanta. The organization had grown too big in its mission and activities for the president to run our day-to-day activities and responsibilities on a part-time basis. He could not be at his job or place of business and at the 100's office at the same time. This was particularly clear to me because when I was president, I was often in the 100's office for thirty hours a week, not at my job where I also had important responsibilities.

We decided that we should hire an Executive Director/Chief Operating Officer. When we began our search, we did not intend to employ a member of the because we felt it would be a conflict of interest. However, at the end of the search, the candidates were both members: John T. Grant, Jr. and Lenny Springs. John was living in Atlanta, but Lenny, who had been in the third class of the 100, had moved his membership to Charlotte after a job transfer in 1999.

After several meetings, we selected John Grant for the position. John was an excellent choice because he was intimately familiar with every aspect of the organization, and he had already proven through his work with the students that he was totally dedicated to our cause. Since he was hired, John has led the charge to move our organization forward.

John T. Grant, Jr.

Executive Director & COO
100 Black Men of Atlanta, Inc.

    I started working for Airborne Express when I was a sophomore at North Carolina A&T State University. After working my way up through the ranks of corporate America, I really thought I would retire from Airborne in a few years. When the position of Executive Director and Chief Operating Officer became available at the 100 Black Men of Atlanta, I heard a call that reminded me of something I had experienced as a child growing up in North Carolina.

    My siblings and I had to work in the community and at the church with my father and mother. My father later became a preacher. We were always helping people and spending all day at church on Sundays. Daddy called it giving back. That's what I wanted to do with my life: give back.

    Since becoming COO of the 100, I can still hear my Daddy getting ready on Sunday mornings to give back at church. Now when I get up in the morning, I understand as a man what he was trying to do. This is not a position where you can think about climbing a corporate ladder. Everything you do is for the children. You cannot think about your next raise or who you did not call back on a given day. You think about the difference you and your staff can make in a child's life.

    I'm glad I listened to the call. I'm glad the 100 Black Men of Atlanta listened also.

Ramon M. (Ray) Singer
Programs Manager, 100 Black Men of Atlanta, Inc.

John Grant is one of the most dedicated people I have ever met. He is driven daily to make this organization better. When he interviewed me for the position of Programs Manager, I knew I wanted to work under his leadership and help with the students of Project Success. John wanted me to know that my job was not going to be a cakewalk. Neither he nor I can turn off our cell phones and pretend the students don't exist until nine o'clock in the morning. We can't walk out of the office at 5:00 clock, or leave the job behind when we finally do go home. The students need our help twenty-four hours a day.

I have a family of my own, and sometimes because of my commitment to them I have to say no to a student's family. As the Programs Manager, I try to be there when they call.

This year was probably the most challenging because we were preparing to select the new students for Project Success Phase IV. We had over seventy-four students apply for fifty-six slots.

They come to their interviews with so much hope in their eyes. The 9th grade students that we committed to have many opportunities ahead of them in the ensuing four years. The 4th graders have an even greater opportunity because we all have more time to help them to develop their academic and social lives. We have more time to make the best of their chance to do the right thing for their future.

What they all need to understand is they have a chance for a good education if they try. We have students from Phase III who are working now to get back in school after making mistakes that caused them to have to leave college.

Phillip Thompson
Project Success Phase III

I want to go back to college in the spring of 2006 to finish the two years that I need to graduate. I should be graduating that year, but I dropped out after two years at Alabama State University.

I had the same opportunity as all the other students in Project Success, and I had the best mentor, Archie Hill, that anyone could ask for. Mr. Hill is the only father I have ever had in my entire life.

I was fortunate enough to get into Project Success because my mother moved my sister and me to Atlanta when I was ten to get us away from Chicago. Not just from Chicago, but the roughest housing projects you can imagine. She wanted us to live in a safer environment and get a good education.

I met Mr. Hill while I was attending the Upward Bound Program where he was a volunteer. Although I left school, Mr. Hill has continued to be supportive. He is never too far away if I need him. He truly cares about my family and me. It is my hope that I can re-enroll in school next spring and make him as proud of me as I am to be his mentee.

Bernard M. Porché

As Ray Singer joined the organization, I was leaving my post as president and Bill Stanley was assuming the mantle. All of the things that I set out to do with Jim George were not done, but at least they were in motion.

The most important thing we, as members of the 100, must understand about what we do is that our actions and decisions will impact the students. We started out as an organization to help students get an education, but we ended up fathers, friends, and family members. For that I am proud. No one better than Bill Stanley could have carried on the mission.

William J. Stanley, III

When I joined this organization, I wanted to serve my community and mentor the students who needed us.

After serving on the Board of the 100 Black Men as a representative of my company, Stanley, Love, Stanley, P.C., my wife and I thought I could bring a new level of business management to the 100 Black Men of Atlanta as we made a greater financial commitment to the Phase III students and the Project Success Phase IV. I felt we needed to approach each of our "events" as a business unit. We needed to expand their potential, leverage of sponsorship, and expand the entire week of the Atlanta Football Classic.

I also felt a strong sense of commitment to this organization because of my own ties to the Atlanta community. I am a fourth generation Atlantan, and I graduated in 1966 from Archer High School (known then as Samuel H. Archer Comprehensive High School).

One of the first tasks on my agenda as president was to make sure that the Family & Youth Empowerment Program was taken to another level. After years of working to assist in bettering the lives of the young people in Project Success, we realized that if we could empower their parents with better lives, we could empower the children. The Family & Youth Empowerment Program partnered with Fannie Mae to help the parents become first-time homebuyers. The parents would deposit money into an account at Fannie Mae until they had a total of $1,500 in their account. This was not only a method to help some of the students move into better neighborhoods, but also to teach them that they could save money and have a house of their own one day. It took some time to get the program off the ground, but in 2005, our first parents, Thomas and Vanessa Bailey, moved into their new home.

The Bailey Family celebrating after Mrs. Bailey was named Para Professional of the Year at William Boyd Elementary School, 2004. (Left to right) Damone Bailey, Thomas Bailey, Vanessa Bailey, Whitney Bailey and Candice Bailey. Candice is a Project Success Phase III student and a freshman at Clark Atlanta University.

LETTER FROM THE BAILEY FAMILY

Dear 100 Black Men of Atlanta, Inc.

The Family & Youth Empowerment Program has allowed us to realize our dream of home ownership. We can't tell you what a wonderful feeling that is.

Your Program's many seminars and workshops provided an opportunity to meet a number of key people in decision-making positions who would ultimately become our friends, and have an interest in helping us make our dream come true. Many times the road to home ownership is difficult, not because of the strict lending guidelines in place to protect lenders, but because the lenders don't really get to know their clients. Through your Program, we were able to meet a great group of providers, vendors, and specialists that we would not have met on our own. They really took the time to get to know us as individuals and not just another loan number. They became good friends and allies during our home buying experience and beyond. The Program allowed plenty of time for us to get to know each other in a friendly environment where we could establish personal relationships, relationships that were used to evaluate our character and not just our numbers when it came time to finance our home.

Your group took a personal interest in us and really wanted us to succeed. The 100 was willing to step in and help whenever we needed them, and they did it because they wanted to help a friend, a friend they met during the many evening and weekend workshops we attended.

Thank you 100 Black Men of Atlanta, as well as the providers and lenders, for being such good friends and helping us achieve our dream home.

The Baileys
Thomas, Vanessa, Damone, Whitney and Candice

Like an octopus in a sea of opportunity, the 100 Black Men of Atlanta have continued to put its tentacles around students by providing love, leadership, and motivation.

Bobby L. Olive
Vice President for Student Affairs
Atlanta Metropolitan College
Board Member, 100 Black Men of Atlanta, Inc.

William J. Stanley, III

The Family & Youth Empowerment Program also gives parents access to the 100 Resource Learning Center. This center is mainly for our students, but we offer computer classes for the parents as well.

After relocating our headquarters to the historic Herndon Plaza at 100 Auburn Avenue, the space that previously housed our office at 35 Broad Street was converted into the 100 Resource Learning Center (100 RLC), a state of the art computer resource center. There the students have access to the Internet, tutors, college resource books and, most of all, a staff of teachers and counselors to help them. Consultant and IT expert, Don Whitley has done a tremendous job over the past three years to keep both the office and the 100 RLC up to date with modern technology.

We were extremely grateful in 2004 when one of our members, Steven W. Smith, Vice President of Corporate Responsibility at Turner Broadcasting System, secured a $500,000 donation to be used for the 100 Resource Learning Center. This donation has helped us continue to provide many valuable services to our students and their parents.

With the 100 RLC in place, John Grant at the helm of the day-to-day operation, and the largest staff in the history of the organization, I felt good about leaving office. Like Bernard and I had done before, Robert G. Haley and I developed a very close relationship as he became our 10th president and as Darrell Fitzgerald became president-elect.

Having a full-time competent executive director and a dedicated staff are among the reasons why I even considered serving as president of the 100. John Grant was the right executive director at the right time in our development. Many of our past presidents had given the organization all the attention it deserved, but more than they actually had to give. It was a full time job for many of them and I commend them for making the sacrifices they made for the young people and this community.

But what John brought to the table was a first. Few of our members have shown the loyalty that he has continuously shown for seventeen years. John and I joined the organization in the same class, and Bob and I had worked together on various community projects before becoming president and president-elect. Darrell Fitzgerald and I had worked together on a number projects and I was well aware of his ability to lead. Darrell donated a great deal of his time and energy to designing the office space for our staff, and he has also been there for the students when they needed assistance.

He was a member at the time, not president-elect, so I feel his gesture simply meant he cared. He came in with a team from his office and not only designed the space, but he went to corporate America and asked for donations for furnishings for the new office and the 100 RLC.

Karen D. Roberts

The 100 Resource Learning Center was a challenge to say the least when it served as our office space. There were days when we were afraid to turn the microwave on at lunch time for fear that the computers would shut down. We didn't have the partitions and nice furniture that we have today.

When we did find our home at 100 Auburn Avenue, Bank of America informed us that we could continue using the space at 35 Broad Street, we were thrilled. Darrell worked hard to make the 100 Resource Learning Center what you see today when you walk in the door. There are working computers everywhere. The staff and teachers have office space and the necessary tools to further educate our children and parents.

(left-right) Office Manager Karen D. Roberts, Gloria S. Ellison, Events Coordinator and Kenya N. Summerour, Senior Programs Associate, working in the conference room at the office of the 100 Black Men of Atlanta.

Member Steven W. Smith, Sr. spends time with students at the 100 Resource Learning Center.

100 Black Men of Atlanta, Inc.'s Professional Staff:
(Front row left to right) John T. Grant, Jr., Executive Director & Chief Operating Officer; Kenya N. Summerour, Senior Programs Associate; Gwendolyn Ball Julien, Finance Manager; Gloria S. Ellison, Events Coordinator; Diane Davis Waugh, Development Director; Nannette Wilson, Executive Assistant; Otis T. Threatt, Jr., Accounting, IT & Events Assistant. (Back row left to right) Karen D. Roberts, Office Manager and Ramon M. Singer, Programs Manager.

Darrell A. Fitzgerald, FAIA
President Elect, 100 Black Men of Atlanta, Inc.
Principal, Gensler Architecture and Planning Worldwide

Designing the office for the 100 Black Men of Atlanta was not just another project for me. Juan Montier who is a member and interior designer worked hard with me to shape a home for the staff that worked daily to enrich the lives of the young people in Project Success. It was more than business for me. It was my duty as a member and as a product of the effect good mentoring can have on a young person's life.

During the first eleven years of my life, my family lived in public housing, but I had good parents in the home with me. They were open to other people helping their children better their lives. I remember coming home from school one day and my mother said "Darrell how would you like to go to prep school." I was 14 and I said, "Okay Ma, but what is prep school?" She explained to me that prep school is to prepare you for college. She also explained to me that Lawrenceville Preparatory School was founded in 1810, and had never had a black student enrolled.

That moment changed my life. To go from the inner city to Lawrenceville was like a dream. My mother was a bank teller and my father was a detective. They could not afford to send me to Lawrenceville Prep on their salaries.

I took the entrance test and received a full scholarship. The tuition was $3,000 in 1964 and today it is over $30,000. That experience put me on the right academic track.

After I got accepted to Lawrenceville, I had my first experience with mentoring. A man named Mr. William Geer was assigned to tutor me every day for the entire summer before I started at the prep school. I had daily tutoring to prepare me to compete with the other students there.

Twenty years later when I became a fellow in the American Institute of Architects, Mr. Geer read an article about me in the New York Times. He called afterwards and said, "I'm Mr. Geer. Do you remember me?"

"Yes, Mr. Geer, how could I forget you?" I said. "You are the guy who got me ready for Lawrenceville Prep." That is the way I will always remember him.

How do you forget that kind of mentoring, love and devotion that a total stranger gives to you?

That is why I appreciate the 100 so much, and why I appreciate the students in Project Success. I know if these students embrace the gifts the 100 are offering, they will excel.

I also know the students have given a lot to the members. I have a son, but I was only a member of the 100 for a month when I was assigned my mentee, Marcus Williams. Marcus has a great dad who is not an absentee father. He is so concerned about his son that he has never had an ego about the role I play in Marcus' life.

Marcus D. Williams
Project Success Phase III
Freshman, Savannah State University

When Mr. Fitzgerald came into my life, God knew that I would need him. I was only in the program for a few days when my brother Stanley was murdered. I don't remember much about that day. I just remember all the crying, and the people coming to my grandmother's house. Nothing made sense to me. When Mr. Fitzgerald received the bad news that Stanley was dead, he came over immediately. My father was in so much pain, and it was unbearable to watch momma.

Mr. Fitzgerald was careful not to overstep his boundaries, but he asked my Dad if I could go home with him. It was the best thing for me, and my Dad knew it. He gave Mr. Fitzgerald his consent. When we arrived at Mr. Fitzgerald's house we just sat around and talked. We ate and at some point I fell asleep. When I woke, Mr. Fitzgerald was right there for me. That day, he promised me that he would always be there for me. He has kept that promise, and I am grateful to him, his wife Joy and son Ryan.

No one can ever replace my brother Stanley, but the 100 Black Men of Atlanta are cool. Their love eases the pain.

In Loving Memory Of...

October 22, 1983 - July 23, 2002
Stanley E. Williams

Project Success Phase III
Stephenson High School, 2002
Stanley would have been a Freshman at
Tennessee State University in the fall of 2002.

Darrell A. Fitzgerald

I wanted to be Marcus' mentor because I have been fortunate enough to have people guiding me all of my life. Because of that, I feel it is my duty to be a member of the 100 Black Men of Atlanta. Anything and everything we do should ultimately go back to our primary goal of helping to enrich the lives of young people.

Marcus is a freshman in college. Because he wants to succeed, we are willing to help him in any way we can. Through hard work and dedication, he has improved his grades from Cs and Ds to As and Bs.

I am very proud of Marcus. I am also very proud of my own son, Ryan, for his willingness to share me with Marcus. I have never felt that it was not okay with Ryan or my wife, Joy, to mentor Marcus. Their love and support has helped me to be a better mentor.

I will always look at mentoring Marcus as my number one role as a member of the 100. All of the members should have a mentee, and they should take that role seriously.

Being president-elect gives being a member of the 100 Black Men of Atlanta a whole new meaning. I think Sonny Walker explained it best when he said that serving as president of the 100 is an eight-year commitment. It starts with the two years or more you use as time to prepare to campaign for president-elect. Serving as president-elect is a commitment of being there for your president on one hand, and preparing to be president on the other.

The two years you serve as president is both demanding and rewarding. When your term is over, you still have a two- year advisory role to serve as president emeritus. It is important to understand the commitment of those eight years before you start campaigning.

As Robert Haley prepares to leave office, I look forward to serving as president of the 100 Black Men of Atlanta. I look forward to the challenge and the commitment.

My dad is always trying to help other people. My mother and I were not surprised when he joined the 100 Black Men of Atlanta and came home with a new family member. I like Marcus a lot. It was really sad when his brother died, so we became brothers and friends.

Ryan Fitzgerald
Darrell Fitzgerald's son

President elect Darrell A. Fitzgerald accompanied by his mentee, Marcus Williams enjoy the Project Success Holiday Celebration at Magic Johnson Theatre in Atlanta, Georgia, December 2002.

Robert G. Haley
President, 100 Black Men of Atlanta, Inc.
Director of National Initiatives, Georgia Institute of Technology

It is truly an honor to be president of the 100 Black Men of Atlanta as we celebrate our 20th Anniversary. I joined this organization in 1991, when Joe Hoffman was still president.

My journey with the 100 started when Collier St. Clair, who died in February, 2002, asked me to join. When he told me about Project Success, I knew that this was the right organization for me. I wanted to be a part of an organization that focused on our youth and on their education.

I immediately joined the Atlanta Football Classic committee, which was only three years old, but already an institution in Atlanta. Within months of joining the organization, I witnessed our Project Success Phase I students graduate from high school and make plans for college. It was a very rewarding experience, and I knew I had become a part of an organization that would make a difference in the lives of young people for generations to come.

After I attended the Phase I students' graduation, I wanted to increase my involvement with the organization. Therefore, I campaigned to become treasurer. That would require me to serve four years under the Dossman and Dortch administrations.

The years I spent working on the various committees prepared me to one day seek election as president of the 100. I believe that one must serve before seeking the highest office of any organization. It was very important to me during the early years to understand the function of each committee and its mission.

When I became president-elect, William Stanley and I organized our second Strategic Plan for the organization with the assistance of the Carl Vinson Institute. This new Strategic Plan will serve as our guide for the next eight years.

We also had the responsibility of the Phase IV class, and I knew it was going to take a large amount of money to operate our Saturday School and 100 Academy as well as pay our students' post-secondary education costs. In addition to our Strategic Plan, we officially launched a $7.2 million campaign in February 2005.

Diane D. Waugh has been the Development Director for the 100 for two years. She has done a wonderful job organizing this campaign.

Diane Davis Waugh
Development Director
100 Black Men of Atlanta, Inc.

I always tell people that I did not find this job, it found me. And for that, I am glad. I was ready for a career change when the employment service I was using told me about the position with the 100. When I interviewed with John Grant, I knew this job was the position for me.

There was just this connection as far back as my childhood in New York. My father had many friends who were members of the New York chapter back in the 60s. I was aware of their cause and how much they cared about our children. As a mother, I understand the importance of caring for our youth.

So when we started our campaign, I was ready to tell sponsors why they should join us in securing the education of Project Success. We launched the Project Success Community Campaign in February 2005, with a breakfast at the 191 Club in Atlanta, Georgia. Our co-chairs, Phil Kent, from Turner Broadcasting System and Felker W. Ward, Jr. from Pinnacle Investment Advisors both spoke. They led the charge to help us reach our goal. The 100 Black Men of Atlanta announced their commitment to raise the initial four million dollars.

With twelve dedicated committee members, we have reached eighty percent of our goal to date. Our corporate sponsors, new and old, understand what we are doing to make a difference in the lives of youth. Changing a generation.

Ingrid Saunders Jones
Senior Vice President, Corporate External Affairs
The Coca-Cola Company & Chairperson
The Coca-Cola Foundation

Since 1987, I have been a supporter and a sponsor for Project Success. Before joining The Coca-Cola Company, I was a school teacher, so I know the daily struggle of trying to educate a child. We have a responsibility as parents, teachers, politicians, and corporate leaders to give all we can to our youth.

One of the first components that Coca-Cola looks for when an organization asks for their assistance is the long-term goal of what the finances will be used for. The 100 Black Men of Atlanta have always been clear about where they are going and what they will do with the funds Coca-Cola donates to Project Success.

It is hard to believe that it has been twenty years since the 100 started this journey. We are proud to partner with this wonderful organization, and to be a part of the lives of young people who will one day hold positions in corporate America. We hope our support will help them to one day give back some of the mentoring and financial support that they have received to help other children.

The 100 is one of the strongest and best examples of men responding effectively to the challenge to lead by example.

Mr. David M. Ratcliffe
Chairman, President & CEO
Southern Company

Robert G. Haley

Today, if a new member were to ask me what would be the best way to serve in this organization, I would tell him that there is no better way than being a mentor. My mentee, April Leonard, came into my life much later than most students who are involved in Project Success. She applied when she was approaching the 12th grade. I cannot tell you how rewarding it has been for me to help April further her education.

April was a student at Dillard University until Hurricane Katrina destroyed most of New Orleans on August 29, 2005, forcing her and over four hundred thousand people to leave Louisiana. She is a brave young lady and she made it back to Atlanta and enrolled at Georgia State University. Without any assistance, April applied for an internship at the Washington Center for Internships and Academic Seminars in Washington, D.C. and she was accepted.

Project Success Phase III student April Leonard shares a moment with her mentor, president Robert G. Haley in Washington, D.C., where she is an intern with the Department of Veterans Affairs.

April M. Leonard
Project Success Phase III
Junior, Dillard University

When the hurricane came to New Orleans, I was already safe at home in Atlanta. I was very sad that so many people were killed, and that the city was almost destroyed. However, my mother assured me that everything was going to be all right.

Mr. Haley immediately started helping me to enroll at Georgia State University. I stayed there only a few days before I was accepted at The Washington Center for Internships and Academic Seminars. Mr. Haley flew with me to Washington, D.C. to help me get settled. I feel so blessed to have the mother and the mentor that I have, and to be a Project Success student. In the worst of times, they are there for me.

I didn't begin in Phase III like most of the students, but I have tried to never disappoint them for bringing me into their family. One of my friends has been involved in Project Success since she was in the 4th grade. When I submitted my application, I had already missed so many things they provided to the students. Program components such as mentoring from an early age, field trips, and other community activities were just a few of the things I missed. However, I did participate in the Saturday School where I studied Algebra and Chemistry my last year of high school. Saturday School gave me the opportunity to brush up on a lot of things I had simply forgotten before going off to college.

Dillard University in New Orleans was one of my first choices. It is a small school and that is what I was looking forward to experiencing. It is a place where I could receive more attention to help me stay in good academic standing. I am still a 4.0 student and I enjoy college life.

Having Mr. Haley, as my mentor has been a gift from God. Mr. Haley cares about me, and what happens to me. He helps with my school supplies and encourages my mother and I to stay focused on my ultimate goal: to receive a college education.

I am an only child and it was always my intention, and my mother Gloria Leonard's intention, for me to go to college. The blessing is that we have not had to deal with how to pay for my education. That alone is a load off of my mother, and it allows me to focus on my grades. Many of my friends have no idea how they will pay their tuition. I have not had to think about that since I was selected to join Project Success.

When I complete my college education, I will return to Atlanta and attend graduate school at Emory University. I also plan to continue my volunteer work in the Big Brothers Big Sisters Program.

Because I am so blessed to have a mentor, before the hurricane I always made certain that I visited with my mentee who is a ten-year-old girl in New Orleans. I would sit in class with her and see how she was doing. We talked a lot and sometimes I would take her to McDonald's. I enjoyed her company.

It's important to me to give back. That is what the 100 Black Men of Atlanta for young people everyday.

From mentoring and tutoring to funding college educations, the 100 Black Men of Atlanta does much for Atlanta's disadvantaged youth, and the Woodruff Foundation applauds and supports its effort to do more.

Charles McTier
President, Woodruff Foundation

Robert G. Haley

I am very proud of April as she continues her education in Washington, D.C. Even after the trauma of the hurricane, she glitters with excitement about her education and the life ahead of her.

As I prepare to leave office as the 10th president of the 100 Black Men of Atlanta, I have some sadness because the job is never finished. Over the past twenty years many changes have occurred in all areas and aspects of our society. While 100 Black Men of Atlanta has witnessed much success over this period of time it too must change to keep pace. Taking a cue from the Best Seller *Good to Great* by Jim Collins the Board of Directors began to chart a new course that will insure the viability and sustainability of the mission for the next twenty years. All of this will be implemented under the outstaanding leadership of John Grant and the dedication and commitment of the staff. They are the driving force that allows the organization to realize its potential. We all knew when we launched our second community campaign in February 2005 that it is our responsibility to the young people of Project Success to have a successful campaign to insure that the students will receive the education they deserve. The students enrolled in Project Success Phase IV signed their covenant on August 27, 2005, and in doing so; they have agreed to do their best to succeed in this program and in life.

Albenny Price, D.C.
Programs Chairman, 100 Black Men of Atlanta, Inc.

It is challenging to be the chairman of the Programs committee. Over seventy-four students applied to join Project Success Phase IV, but we only had fifty-six available slots. Nothing is harder than having to look into the face of an eager young person and his or her parents and know they will not all have the same opportunity. The students who were selected have the opportunity to be a part of something unique.

The 100 has the opportunity to make a difference in their lives as mentors. In my opinion, the mentoring provided by this organization is the most important component of what we do. I have three mentees, and I enjoy spending time with them as much as I do my own child.

These children are waiting for someone to come along and give them a hug or help them with their homework. It is always great when they can get all of these things at home, but we are not here to judge their situation at home. We have to admit that some of their parents are working two jobs just to keep a roof over their heads. When they come home, they are simply too tired to help their own children with homework.

The 100 Black Men of Atlanta will continue to try to give their child help with their homework and a hug. For that I am proud.

Corey D. Atkinson
William M. Boyd Elementary
Project Success Phase IV

I am only nine years old, and I am in the 4th grade. I did not understand what Project Success was when my mother told me that I was in this new program. But after I met with Dr. Price and other members of the 100 Black Men of Atlanta, I started to understand better.

This program is going to be good for my family and me.

I love my mother and she tries hard to be a good mother.

I try to be a good son too. I have a big day every day. We get up early and have breakfast and I am off to school. I try to make good grades.

One of my best friends in the whole world is my principal, Dr. Bettye Wright at Boyd Elementary School. She talks to me every day and tells me that I am a good student.

We do fun things with the 100 Black Men too. They gave us tickets to the Atlanta Football Classic back in September. I had a really nice time.

I am looking forward to other fun things, and I am looking forward to college. After college, I am going to be a scientist. That will make my mother and my mentor very proud.

1891 Johnson Rd.
Atlanta, GA 30318
September 28, 2005

Dear 100 Black Men,
    I wanted to write this letter because of what you did for this school. I want to encourage other students to come to school every day not only to get a reward but so they could learn.
    I really appreciate you all for doing this for my lovely school. I've always wanted to become a member of your group. I hope I could write back to you. Maybe I could meet you and fulfill my dream of becoming a member of your group. Thanks for what you all have done for the William M. Boyd family.

        Your friend,
        Cinwon Whitehead

09/05

For
Mr. Grant & 100 Black Men
of Atlanta,

A sincere note
that expresses my
deepest gratitude
for everything
that you've done.

Thanks Again!

Thank you so much for the tickets to
the Classic for our children, parents, and
staff. Our school's attendance was great
as a result of this great incentive. Can
you believe — 95% our children were
present and on time? !!

God Bless you and the rest of
100 Black Men of Atlanta.
　　Bettye D. Wright - Principal
　　W. M. Boyd Elementary School

154

FAMU player Aubrey Parrish at 2005 Bank of America Atlanta Football Classic.

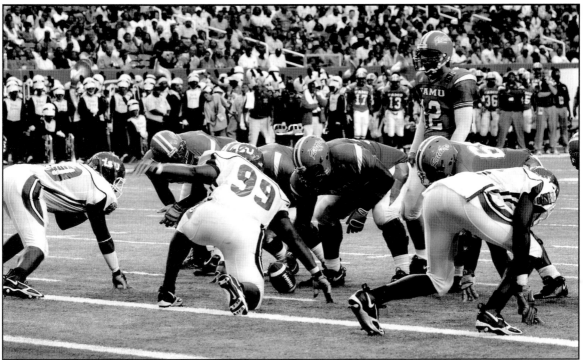

Florida A&M University and Tennessee State University in the Bank of America Atlanta Football Classic, Georgia Dome September 24, 2005.

Member Bobby Olive introduces TSU former President James A. Hefner to members Andrew Young and Hardy Dorsey, Sr. at a reception during the Bank of America Atlanta Football Classic Week.

156

Janal Andrews
(Corey's Mother)

When the letter arrived from the 100 Black Men of Atlanta, my mother Daphine Andrews opened it before I arrived home from work. She called me and told me I had a letter, but she wouldn't tell me what was inside. Of course, I rushed home to read it for myself.

That day was one of the happiest days of my life.

My son is such a good little boy. He wants to learn and do well in life. When that letter arrived, I knew that God had answered my prayers to help my child succeed.

Corey did very well when he was interviewed. I left the interview feeling that my son was definitely going to be accepted, and that he would one day go to college.

Corey knew too. He got up filled with excitement on the morning we were scheduled to sign his covenant. We were all excited. He loves to sleep late on Saturdays, but that day Corey was up at 6:00 a.m. He woke up everybody else in the house too. All the way downtown to the 100's Auburn Avenue office, he filled the car with laughter. I think he was overjoyed at what his future was going to be now that he could one day go to college.

It is hard to raise children today. When people look at you and see you are trying, they will help you. I am so grateful to the 100 for everything that they have done and that they will do for my son, Corey.

We will focus on our mission and our promise, and we will continue our work to ensure that we are here to serve the Atlanta Community today, tomorrow, and for generations to come.

Robert G. Haley
President & Chairman of the Board
100 Black Men of Atlanta, Inc.

Nathaniel R. Goldston, III

It's hard to believe that it has been twenty years since we met at the Mansion Restaurant. It's hard to believe that we are celebrating twenty years of brotherly love and commitment to the young people in Project Success.

Many students have gone through Project Success, graduated from high school and college, and gone out into the world and found good jobs. My mentee, Tony, is thirty-two years old now and he has a twelve-year-old son.

It had been a long time since I had seen Tony, my other son, until Shelia Moses called and told me she needed to talk to him before she could finish writing this book.

Antonio "Tony" Thomas
Project Success Phase I

Mr. Goldston has never forgotten me and I will never forget what he did for my family and me. I failed to stay in touch with him, but he never lost touch with my uncle.

In September 2005, I was visiting my uncle when Mr. Goldston called to ask him to find me because he wanted me to be interviewed for this book. I had not heard his voice in seven years.

Mr. Goldston is a good man. He came into my life when I needed a father figure. My father has always been absent from my life, so my mother welcomed the love that Mr. Goldston gave me.

I was at the age that his presence in my life was a deciding factor in my manhood. He was good to me, but he had rules for me just like he had for his own two sons. He took me with them everywhere they went, and he treated me as a third son.

Growing up in Perry Homes was hard. I had no idea how nice the world was outside of the housing projects. I remember going on trips with Mr. Goldston and his family. I can still remember what the water felt like on my skin the first time I jumped into the pool in his back yard. I did not understand that black people could be this successful and live such good lives.

Everything about being a man I learned from him. He gave me my manhood by teaching me and being a good example of what a man should be.

I am a father now. Mr. Goldston taught me how to be a good father. Every time I think about yelling at my son, I think about his gentle voice. Then, I talk to my son like Mr. Goldston talked to me so many years ago. Quietly, calmly. It makes all the difference in the world.

I am so glad I was sitting on my uncle's porch that day when Mr. Goldston called his house. I am glad that we found each other again.

Nathaniel R. Goldston, III

You never know how much you can help a person until you try. Project Success is only a small fraction of what people in the world can do to help others. There are millions of children just like Tony who can be successful if someone just show them a little love.

The 100 Black Men of Atlanta cannot save the world but, working together, we can try to make a difference. We have truly tried to do, "The Right Thing for the Right Reason."

Founding President Nathaniel R. Goldston, III and Project Success student Robert Page attend the President's Luncheon at the Atlanta Hilton & Towers Hotel, June 8, 1991. Robert is currently attending Atlanta Technical College.

In Loving Memory Of...

Robert W. Allen, Ph.D.
August 31, 1933 - July 23, 2005

Justin L. Johnson
October 28, 1962 - August 21,
2004

Lester W. Butts, Ph.D.
March 30, 1927 - November 6,
1999

Samuel Lightfoot, Sr., M.D.
February 23, 1941 - March 17, 2004

Alonzo A. Crim, Ph.D
October 1, 1928-May 3, 2000

Warner E. Meadows, Jr., M.D.
1931 - 2004

James W. George
March 21, 1948 - October 29, 1999
7th President

Lionel Whaley
July 22, 1951 - July 28, 2005

Maynard H. Jackson
March 23, 1938 - June 23, 2003

George G. Woody, III
July 15, 1952 - October 14, 2004

CHRONOLOGY

1968   100 Black Men founded as an organization in New York. This organization would provide the overall concept behind the 100 Black Men of Atlanta.

1986   The 100 Black Men of Atlanta was founded on February 4, 1986 at the Mansion Restaurant on Piedmont Avenue in Atlanta, Georgia.

Nathaniel R. Goldston, III elected first President of the 100 Black Men of Atlanta and serves from 1986 – 1989.

Joseph I. Hoffman, Jr., M.D. elected as president-elect.

October 10 - Organization incorporated under the State Seal of Georgia by the Secretary of State Max Cleland and became known as the 100 Black Men of Atlanta, Inc.

1987   March - Project Success Phase I, a mentoring and tuition-assistance program collaboration between the 100 Black Men of Atlanta and twenty-seven students at Samuel H. Archer Comprehensive High School in the Perry Homes Community of Atlanta was founded.

May 27 - The first national convention for the 100 Black Men of America, Inc. was held in Atlanta, Georgia and hosted by the newly formed Atlanta chapter.

May 27 - The first Le Cabaret was held at the Westin Peachtree Plaza Hotel in Atlanta, Georgia and featured Phyllis Hyman.

December 1 - Monica B. Douglas hired as first program director for Project Success.

1988 March - The Internal Revenue Service issued the organization's 501(c)(3) determination status.

1989 The Saturday Academy was implemented for Project Success students to help facilitate tutoring, enhance academic skills and develop leadership skills. (Twelve weeks for each academic semester.)

Joseph I. Hoffman, Jr. assumes second presidency of the 100 Black Men of Atlanta, Inc. and serves from 1989 – 1991.

The Atlanta Ebony Classic I fundraiser was held on September 23rd at Georgia Tech's Grant Field Stadium and featured Tennessee State University versus Florida A&M University along with their marching bands.

1990 Second Football Classic, which was renamed Atlanta Football Classic, was held on September 22nd at Georgia Tech's Grant Field and featured Tennessee State University versus Florida A&M University along with their marching bands.

The 100 Black Men of Atlanta, Inc. acquires its first office space located at 615 Peachtree Street, 11th floor, in downtown Atlanta, Georgia.

1991   March 11 - Karen Roberts hired as first office manager for the organization.

William "Sonny" Walker assumes third presidency of the 100 Black Men of Atlanta, Inc. and serves from 1991 – 1993.

Thirty-three of the thirty-five students in Project Success graduated from Archer High School in June 1991. Thirty went on to post-secondary institutions.

Atlanta Football Classic III was held on September 28th at Georgia Tech's Grant Field and featured two new HBCUs, Southern University versus South Carolina State University and their marching bands.

1992   The 100 Black Men of Atlanta, Inc. institutes a multi-stage continuum of Project Success for 4th and 5th grade students attending William E. Boyd, Clara Maxwell Pitts and William J. Scott elementary schools. This program is considered Project Success Phase II and included a "Read to Succeed" component in partnership with Scholastic, Inc.

The first 100 Golf Classic was held April 13th at the Atlanta Athletic Club.

September 19 - Atlanta Football Classic IV was moved to the new Georgia Dome and featured South Carolina State University versus Southern University and their respective marching bands. This game represented the first college football game to be played in the facility.

October - The 100 Black Men of Atlanta, Inc. relocates office into donated space from First Union National Bank located at 127 Peachtree Street, 7th Floor (The Candler Building) in downtown Atlanta.

1993   Thomas W. Dortch, Jr. assumes the fourth presidency of the 100 Black Men of Atlanta, Inc. and serves from 1993 - 1995.

100 Black Men of Atlanta, Inc. publishes its first newsletter entitled "On The Move" with a contribution received through Lincoln-Mercury.

1994   September - First 5K Run/Walk for Success held.

Organization launches its Anti-Violence Campaign entitled "Enough Tears - Stop the Violence" which included three major component areas: Advocacy, Awareness and Demonstration.

1995 Curley M. Dossman, Jr., Esq. assumes the fifth presidency of the 100 Black Men of Atlanta, Inc. and serves from 1995 – 1997.

Organization contracts with Coxe Curry and Associates to implement its first Community Campaign to raise over $2 million for Project Success.

1996 Organization relocates office to 35 Broad Street, 1st Floor in downtown Atlanta through a donation of space from Bank of America.

June - Project Success Phase I students graduate from college.

July - Organization holds unveiling ceremony for Olympic bricks purchased for members and staff commemorating participation in the XXVI Olympiad held in Atlanta, Georgia.

Organization celebrates its ten-year anniversary with a year-long celebration of events and activities commemorating the milestone. A special ten-year anniversary logo is developed.

1997 Raymond J. McClendon assumes the sixth presidency of 100 Black Men of Atlanta, Inc. and serves from 1997 – 1999.

June - Community campaign reached goal of $2 million.

September - Gwendolyn Ball Julien hired as the new Finance Manager.

1998 Kenya N. Summerour hired as the new Senior Programs Associate.

August-September - The 100 Black Men of Atlanta, Inc. officially launch Project Success Phase III with special covenant-signing ceremony attended by students, parents and members of the Atlanta School Board.

Georgia Governor Zell Miller proclaims September 26, 1998 as "100 Black Men of Atlanta Day" in the state of Georgia.

Collegiate 100 of Atlanta founded in order to increase the 100's impact on the students of Project Success and in the community. Collegiate 100 of Atlanta is a group of area college students who have agreed to nurture and enhance the academic achievement and personal growth of the Project Success students while giving back to the community.

1999 James W. George assumes the seventh presidency of the 100 Black Men of Atlanta, Inc. and fulfills only six months of his two-year term after passing away in October due to complications from diabetes. Jim was the first member of the organization to pass away. President Elect Bernard M. Porché completes his unexpired term.

June - The 100 Black Men of Atlanta launch the Points of Hope Program.

The New Stars Volunteer Program is launched.

The Parental Involvement Committee was founded. Charles Waddell was the first chair.

2000   Bernard M. Porché assumes the eighth presidency of the 100 Black Men of Atlanta, Inc. and serves from 2000 – 2002.

Georgia Power becomes Title Sponsor of the Atlanta Football classic and serves through 2003.

2001   November 14 - John T. Grant, Jr. begins his tenure as the new Executive Director and Chief Operating Officer for the 100 Black Men of Atlanta, Inc.

The implementation of the Female Mentoring Project (Girls of Project Success).

2002   William J. Stanley, III, FAIA, NOMA assumes the ninth presidency of the 100 Black Men of Atlanta, Inc. and serves from 2002 – 2004.

Organization resumes publication of its quarterly newsletter and changes name to the "100 Advisor."

March 25 - Ramon M. Singer hired as the new Programs Director for Project Success.

2003   January 2 - Diane Davis Waugh hired as the new Development Director.

April - 100 Black Men of Atlanta, Inc. relocates headquarters to historic Herndon Plaza through donated office from Atlanta Life Financial Group.

Maynard H. Jackson, former Mayor of Atlanta and member of the 100 Black Men of Atlanta, Inc. dies at the age of 65.

July 1 - Otis T. Threatt, Jr. hired as the new Accounting/ IT and Events Assistant. Serving also in the capacity of Collegiate 100 Advisor.

September 20 - The 100 Black Men of Atlanta set a new stadium attendance record with 70,509 alumni and fans at the Atlanta Football Classic. (That record still stands as of the publish date of this book.)

Organization commissions Deloitte to complete a Financial Operational Assessment study.

The Carl Vinson Institute for Government at the University of Georgia provides gratis services to the organization in the creation and development of a new Strategic Plan for the 100.

The 100 Black Men of Atlanta, Inc., in partnership with Turner Broadcasting System, Inc., launches the 100 Resource Learning Center.

2004   Robert G. Haley assumes the tenth presidency of the 100 Black Men of Atlanta, Inc. and serves from 2004 – 2006.

Darrell A. Fitzgerald, FAIA elected as president elect of the 100 Black Men of Atlanta, Inc. and will serve from 2006-2008.

June 23 - Bank of America becomes Title Sponsor of the Atlanta Football Classic.

August 9 - Gloria S. Ellison hired as the new Events Coordinator.

Georgia Power becomes Title Sponsor of the Parade of Excellence.

2005   January - 100 Black Men of Atlanta, Inc. convenes the first 100 Georgia Chapters Summit in Peachtree City, Georgia.

February - Official launch of the Project Success Community Campaign to complete funding of Project Success Phase III and to fund Project Success Phase IV.

August - Organization launches Project Success Phase IV begins consisting of twenty-eight 4th graders and twenty-eight 9thgraders. The 9th graders comprise the 100 Scholars. The organization plans to add twenty-eight new students in both grade levels each year until 2008. The expected completion of Phase IV is 2021.

December - The 100's first book "Project Success - The Right Thing for the Right Reason" by Shelia P. Moses is released.

BIBLIOGRAPHY

Articles and Books

---100 Black Men of Atlanta, Inc. "100 Black Men of Atlanta Announce." Title Sponsor of Annual Football Classic." The Atlanta Inquirer September 22, 2001: Section B. Vol. 41, No. 8.

---"100 Black Men of Atlanta, Incorporated Backgrounder." The Atlanta Inquirer September 22, 2005: Section B. Vol. 41, No. 8.

---"Super Bowl of Black College Football." The Atlanta Inquirer September 22, 2001: Section B. Vol. 42, No. 9.

---"Two Georgia Tech Men Sworn in as President." The Atlanta Inquirer September 28, 2002: Section B. Vol. 42, No. 9.

---"100 Black Men of Atlanta: The Power of Volunteerism Charity Starts At Home." The Atlanta Inquirer September 28, 2002: Section B. Vol. 42, No. 9.

---Grant, John. "100 Black Men of Atlanta-Chief Operating Officer." The Atlanta Inquirer September 28, 2005: Section B. Vol. 42, No. 9.

---"100 Black Men Project Success Summary." The Atlanta Inquirer September 28, 2005: Section B. Vol. 42, No. 9.

PHASE I (1987 – 1996)

Last Name	First Name	Graduated From	Post-Secondary Experience
Almond	Alicia	Samuel Archer High School	Employed
Austin	Fionne	Samuel Archer High School	Spelman College & GA Tech
Bembry	Maco	Samuel Archer High School	Branell Institute
Boss	Freddie	Samuel Archer High School	Employed full-time at HNTB Engineering Firm
Brown	Rodrecas	Samuel Archer High School	Employed
Brown	Tameka	Samuel Archer High School	Clark Atlanta University
Bush	Lolita	Samuel Archer High School	Employed
Carter	Sequetta	Samuel Archer High School	Atlanta Metropolitan College
Copeland	Viondi	Samuel Archer High School	Morehouse College
Crumbley	Elliott	Samuel Archer High School	Clark Atlanta University
Daniels	Desmond	Samuel Archer High School	Southern Polytechnic State University
Davis	Glenn	Samuel Archer High School	Employed
Gunn	Tameka	Samuel Archer High School	Morris College
Jelks	Sonya	Samuel Archer High School	Syracuse University
Jenkins	Derrick	Samuel Archer High School	Voorhees College
Johnson	Alton	Samuel Archer High School	Employed
Johnson	Michelle	Samuel Archer High School	Georgia State University
Johnson	Sheila	Samuel Archer High School	Atlanta Metropolitan College
Lewis	Pamela	Towers High School	Hampton University
Long	Paige	George High School	Atlanta Job Corps
McBride	Lakesha	Samuel Archer High School	National Education Center Mitchell
Lavonia	Samuel	Archer High School	Employed
Murray	Virgil	Samuel Archer High School	Employed
Norwood	Atavism	Samuel Archer High School	Employed
Parks	Kateria	Samuel Archer High School	Employed
Scott	Rosa	Samuel Archer High School	Florida A&M University
Smith	Reginald	Samuel Archer High School	Employed
Stephens	Alphia	Samuel Archer High School	Xavier University
Tanner	Erica	Samuel Archer High School	Clark Atlanta University
Thomas	Antonio	Samuel Archer High School	Employed Construction Worker
Ward	John	Samuel Archer High School	Devry Institute of Technology
Williams	Pamela	Samuel Archer High School	Clark Atlanta University
Williams	Tonya	Samuel Archer High School	Clark Atlanta University

PHASE II and III (1997-Present) : Classes of 2001 and 2002

Last Name	First Name	Graduated From	Post-Secondary Experience
Arnold	Quentendon	Harper-Archer High School	Participation Ended
Baker	Darius	Frederick Douglass High School	Morehouse College
Baxter	Kenneth	Harper-Archer High School	Employed
Belton	April	Harper-Archer High School	Participation Ended
Bryant	LaToya	Harper-Archer High School	Albany State University
Carter	Bianca	McNair Senior High School	Albany State University
Carter	Monica	McNair Senior High School	Florida Culinary Institute
Cousin	Dominique	Frederick Douglass High School	Participation Ended
Fannin	Sheena	Harper-Archer High School	Participation Ended
Few	Arthur	North Atlanta High School	Morehouse College
Forbes	Kurt	Harper-Archer High School	Participation Ended
Franks	Johnathan	Harper-Archer High School	Alabama A&M University
Hart	Branden	Harper-Archer High School	Participation Ended
Hendrix	Candice	Frederick Douglass High School	Participation Ended
Hodges	India	Harper-Archer High School	Alabama A&M University
Humphrey	Devin	Harper-Archer High School	Clark Atlanta University
Jones	Marcus	Frederick Douglass High School	Georgia State University
Jordan	Shereka	Southside Comprehensive High School	Medix School
Lee	LeFabione	Youth Challenge Academy	Atlanta Metropolitan College
Little	April	Frederick Douglass High School	Albany State University
Lowe	Star	Harper-Archer High School	Clark Atlanta University
Marshall	Goldie	Harper-Archer High School	Medix School
Martin	Brian	Frederick Douglass High School	Participation Ended
Rawls	Shavon	Harper-Archer High School	Atlanta Technical College
Smith	Kenneisha	Harper-Archer High School	Albany State University
Thompson	Phillip	Harper-Archer High School	Employed
Walker	Canzata	Chamblee High School	Georgia Perimeter College
Weathersby	Alicia	North Atlanta High School	Clark Atlanta University
Wells	Ahmad	Harper-Archer High School	Employed
White	Dennis	Harper-Archer High School	Tennessee State University
White	Tykiesha	Atlanta Metropolitian College	Advanced Career Training
Williams, Jr.	Stanley	Stephenson High School	Deceased

PHASE II and III(1997-Present) : Class of 2003

Last Name	First Name	Graduated From	Post-Secondary Experience
Armstrong	Rodniqua	Frederick Douglass High School	Georgia State University
Arnold	Shabrekia	North Atlanta High School	Fort Valley State University
Arnold	Shanekia	North Atlanta High School	Fort Valley State University
Bentley	Lakisha	Frederick Douglass High School	Georgia Healthcare Institute
Brandy	Jesse	Frederick Douglass High School	Savannah State University
Cofer	Diontae	Douglass High School-enrolled	Employed
Dunn	Tristan	Frederick Douglass High School	Medix School
Echols, Jr.	Derrick	Frederick Douglass High School	Clemson University
Gamble	Douglas	Frederick Douglass High School	Tennessee State University
Glaze	Willie	Frederick Douglass High School	Dillard University
Goodson	Courtland	Frederick Douglass High School	Georgia Tech University
Julien	Jason	Westlake High School	Florida A & M University
Leonard	April	Frederick Douglass High School	Dillard University
Marshall	Angela	Frederick Douglass High School	Medix School
McCarthy	Steven	Banneker High School	Hampton University
Pollard	Kareem	Frederick Douglass High School	Savannah State University
Robinson	Howard	Frederick Douglass High School	Morehouse College
Simmons	Alan	Frederick Douglass High School	Participation Ended
Tolen	Jessica	Frederick Douglass High School	Tennessee State University

PHASE II and III (1997-Present) : Class of 2004

Last Name	First Name	Graduated From	Post-Secondary Experience
Andrews	Kimberly	Frederick Douglass High School	Employed
Barber	Meeka	Frederick Douglass High School	Georgia Medical Institute
Blount	Keldrin	North Atlanta High School	Hampton University
Carten	Jazmine	Washington High School	Alabama A&M University
Dozier	Shameka	Benjamin E. Mays High School	Atlanta Metropolitan College
Ellington	Christina	Frederick Douglass High School	Xavier University
Harris	Christopher	Frederick Douglass High School	Atlanta Technical College
Hightower	Rasheed	Frederick Douglass High School	Participation Ended
Johnson	Shanika	D. M. Therrell High School	Savannah State University
Love	Christopher	North Atlanta High School	Employed
Mayes	Shaquovious	Benjamin E. Mays High School	United States Army
McGinty	Erika	Frederick Douglass High School	Hampton University
Page	Robert	Frederick Douglass High School	Atlanta Technical College
Randolph	Sharde'	Booker T. Washington High School	Xavier University
Riggins	Benny	North Atlanta High School	Atlanta Metropolitan College
Robinson	Shantae'	Frederick Douglass High School	Spelman College
Snead	Dionne	D. M. Therrell High School	Employed
Thompson	Precious	North Atlanta High School	Medix School

PHASE II and III (1997-Present) : Class of 2005

Last Name	First Name	Graduated From	Post-Secondary Experience
Aghedo	Marcques	Southside Comprehensive High School	Morehouse College
Bailey	Candice	Mays High School	Georgia State University
Banks	Latisha	Frederick Douglass High School	Clark Atlanta University
Barnes	Orion	Frederick Douglass High School	Bethune Cookman College
Burson	Walter	Southside Comprehensive High School	Tuskgee University
Creamer	Shondrecia	Benjamin E. Mays High School	Bauder College
Dennis	Delmonte	Frederick Douglass High School	Bethune Cookman College
Dunn	Christen	Frederick Douglass High School	Employed
Fears	Kalyndria	Southside Comprehensive High School	Albany State University University
Glass	Crystal	Southside Comprehensive High School	Albany State University University
Hall	DeJarvis	Southside High School - Enrolled	Home
Hughes	Corderious	Mays High School	Savannah State University
Lakes	Alexander	Frederick Douglass High School	Morehouse College
Lundy	Antionette	Frederick Douglass High School	Home
Miller	Christopher	Washington High School	Fort Valley State University
Miller	Shawndria	Southside Comprehensive High School	Albany State University
Parker	Dontae	Frederick Douglass High School	Georgia Southern University
Peters	Antoinette	Therrell High School	Atlanta Metropolitan College
Polk	Donald	North Atlanta High School	Atlanta Technical College
Simmons	Nitrecus	Southside Comprehensive High School	Bennett College
Stanley	Benton	North Atlanta High School	Atlanta Metropolitan College
Stanley	Brenton	North Atlanta High School	Atlanta Metropolitan College
Tate	Santana	Southside Comprehensive High School	Clayton College and State University
Tenner	Joseph	Frederick Douglass High School	Bethune-Cookman College
Thomas	Jevon	Frederick Douglass High School	West Point United States Military Academy
Walker	Shatekela	Chamblee High School	Georgia Perimeter College
Whaley	Patrice	Frederick Douglass High School	Paine College
Williams	Marcus	Stephenson High School	Savannah State University

PHASE IV : 4th Grade Students

Last Name	First Name	Elementary School
Atkinson	Corey	William M. Boyd Elementary School
Becnel	Aarionne	Deerwood Academy
Brown	Cherrika	William M. Boyd Elementary School
Cain	Jamario	Parkside Elementary
Carson	Alexander	Deerwood Academy
Clark, Jr.	Domonic	Deerwood Academy
Gordon	Widdie	Deerwood Academy
Hazuri	Hasan	Parkside Elementary
Hendricks	Ashleigh	William M. Boyd Elementary School
Hill	Cierra	William M. Boyd Elementary School
Hill	JaStacckyanna	William M. Boyd Elementary School
Jessie	Justin	Deerwood Academy
Landrum	Maurice	William M. Boyd Elementary School
Lawson	Jerrode	Deerwood Academy
Loyd	Nadeia	Deerwood Academy
Parks	M'Quita	Deerwood Academy
Peters	Breana	Drew Charter Elementary
Phillips	Gregory	Burgess Peterson Elementary
Porter	Shadrian	William M. Boyd Elementary School
Raines	SeVarius	Avondale Elementary School
Robbs	Myreon	Drew Charter Elementary
Smith	Austin	Fairview Elementary School
Smith	Michael	Drew Charter Elementary
Smith	Shadarian	Deerwood Academy
Thrash	Pauleah	Deerwood Academy
Tyler	Jalen	Marshall Elementary
Wise	Clarence	Deerwood Academy
Wise	Shakaria	Deerwood Academy

PHASE IV : 100 Black Men of Atlanta Scholars
Class of 2009

Last Name	First Name	High School
Acree	DeMarcus	Booker T. Washington High School
Bolston	Delandra	Southside Comprehensive High School
Brown	Jametrice	Frederick Douglass High School
Carr	Charles	Frederick Douglass High School
Edwards	Demetruis	Carver Early College
Harris	Dewitt	Frederick Douglass High School
Hines	Diedrick	Henry Grady High School
Jean-Pierre	Naomi	Southside Comprehensive High School
Johnson	Jeffrey	The Padeia School
Jones	Shanquesia	Southside Comprehensive High School
Lindsay	Cedric	Southside Comprehensive High School
Little	Quartez	Miller Grove High School
Lucious	Muhammad	Carver Science & Technology
McCullough	Brenton	Southside Comprehensive High School
Moore	Jasmine	Frederick Douglass High School
Patterson	Conterris	Frederick Douglass High School
Perry, Jr.	Kenneth	Booker T. Washington High School
Perry	Malcolm	Henry Grady High School
Peters	Douglas	Carver Early College
Releford	Jamal	The Lovett School
Rucker	Christian	Jackson High School
Sanford	Crystal	Henry Grady High School
Simpson	Iesha	Henry Grady High School
Souder	Antonika	Frederick Douglass High School
Walker	Mattaura	Booker T. Washington High School
Westbrooks	Bryan	D.M. Therrell High School
Wise	Chauntalia	Benjamin E. Mays High School

100 Black Men of Atlanta, Inc. and the students of Project Success would like to thank the following for their support…

7-11

97.1 JAMZ

100 Black Men of America, Inc.

104.5 FM

107.5. WJZZ

790 The Zone

Aaron Rents, Inc.

Accent Printing Company

Acuity Brands

Abbott Laboratories

Adams Outdoor Advertising

Advanced Systems Technology

AETC

Aetna Foundation

Aetna, Inc.

Airport Information Systems

Airport Shuttle Bus Management
    Association

AGL Resources

Alliance Orthopaedics & Sports
    Medicine

All-Pro Produce Company

Allstate Foundation

Allstate Insurance

Alumax

American Airlines

American Express

American Express Foundation

American Golf

American International Group

American Media Corporation

America's Favorite Chicken

AmeriPark

Anheuser-Busch Companies

Antioch Baptist Church

AOL Black Voices.com

Apex Mortgage Group, Inc.

Apple Computer

Aramark Aviation Service

Arby's

Archer Community Evening High
    School

Armstrong

Arthur Anderson & Company

AstraZeneca LP

Atlanta Braves

Atlanta Civic Center

Atlanta Committee for the Olympic
    Games

Atlanta Convention & Visitors
    Bureau

Atlanta Falcons

Atlanta Foundation

Atlanta Hawks

Atlanta Hilton & Towers

Atlanta Housing Authority

Atlanta Life Financial Group

Atlanta Livery Company

Atlanta Medical Center
Atlanta Metropolitan College
Atlanta Motor Speedway
Atlanta Paint & Body Works
Atlanta Paralympic Organizing
    Committee
Atlanta Public Schools
Atlanta Recreational Authority
Atlanta Sports Council
Atlanta Symphony Orchestra
Atlanta Thrashers
Atlanta Tribune Magazine
Atlantic Business Systems
AT&T
AT&T Broadband
A-Watkins Limousine Service
Bank of America
Bank of America Foundation
Bass Hotels & Resorts
Beers Construction Company
Bellsouth Corporation
Bellsouth Mobility
Bellsouth Foundation
Ben Carson Science Academy
Berry College
Better Brands
BFI
Black Entertainment Television
Blue Cross Blue Shield of Georgia
Bovanti
Burger King Corporation
Butler Street YMCA – Northwest

Byrd Alliance
Café Echelon
Capital Grille
Capitol Outdoor Advertising
Carl E. Sanders
Carl Sams/RattlerTickets.com
Carl Vinson Institute of Government
    (UGA)
Carnegie
Carson Products
Cascade Family Skating Rink
Center for Urban Educational
    Excellence
Charles Schwab
Chase Home Finance
Checkers
Chick-Fil-A
Cigna Healthcare of Georgia
Citizens Trust Bank
City of Atlanta
Clara M. Pitts Elementary School
Clark Atlanta University School of
    Social Work
Classic Soul 102.5
CoatTail Productions, Inc.
Coca-Cola Enterprises
Coca-Cola Fountain
Colgate-Palmolive Company
Comcast
Community Foundation for Greater
    Atlanta
Constangy, Brooks & Smith, LLC

Consumer Credit Counseling Service
Coors Brewing Company
Corey Advertising, Inc.
Country Lake
Courts Foundation, Inc.
Cousins / New Market Development
Crown Distributing Company
Crowne Plaza Ravinia
Countrywide Home Loans, Inc.
Crystal Springs
Dave Simpson Insurance
David, Helen & Marian Woodward
   Fund
Deloitte
Delta Air Lines Foundation
Delta Air Lines, Inc.
DieHard
Digital Telecom, Inc.
Dillard University
Diversified Health Solutions
Diversapack
Dobbs-Paschal Midfield Corporation
Dominos Pizza
Don Coleman & Associates
Dorsey Management Group
Dr. Pepper
Dust-Away, Inc.
Earthkeepers
Eastern Airlines
East Lake Community Foundation
Ebony Glass & Mirror
Eckerd Corporation Foundation

Effective Network Solutions
EDM Industries
Elarbee, Thompson, Sapp & Wilson,
   LLP
ELV Associates, Inc.
Emory University
Empire Distributors
Equitele, Inc.
Ernst & Young
ESPN Zone
Eventions, Inc.
EWA Beverage Group
E.W. Bowen & Company
Expo Africa
Extended Community Home Health
   Care-Atlanta
Fannie Mae
Fannie Mae Foundation
Fashion Shows Unlimited
Federal Express
Federated Insurance
Fijitsu
Film Fabricators
Financial Consulting Associates, Inc.
Fine and Block
First Union National Bank
Fletcher Martin Ewing
Florence & Harry English Memorial
   Fund
Florida A&M University
Ford Foundation
Ford Motor Company

Fortis Family Insurance

Foster Hollowell

Fox Theatre

Frances L. Abreu Charitable Trust

Frank Johnson Lincoln Mercury

Frazier & Deeter, C.P.A.

F T Mortgage Companies

Fulton County

Fulton County Sheriff's Department

G4 Enterprises

Gannett Foundation

GCTV

General Electric

General Mills

General Motors Corporation

Gensler Architecture & Planning
    Worldwide

Genysis

George W. Jenkins Foundation, Inc.

Georgia Army National Guard

Georgia Black United Fund

Georgia Cable Television

Georgia Department of Human
Resources / Division of Family &
Children's Services

Georgia Department of Labor

Georgia Dome

Georgia Environmental Organization

Georgia Golf Promotions

Georgia Institute of Technology

Georgia Lottery Corporation

Georgia-Pacific Corporation

Georgia-Pacific Foundation

Georgia Power Company

Georgia Power Foundation

Georgia Power Network
    Underground Facility

Georgia State University

Georgia State University Athletics

Georgia World Congress Center

GlobalTech Financial

Golden Limousine, Inc. (Detroit)

Good News

Goodrum Enterprises

Gordon Gin

Gourmet Services, Inc.

Graphic Development

Grassroots Promotions, LLC

Hardees Food System, Inc.

Harland Charitable Foundation

Harold A. Dawson

Harper-Archer High School

Hartsfield Hospitality, LLC

Hartsfield-Jackson Atlanta
International Airport

Heineken

HELP, Inc.

Hennessy Lexus

Heritage Cadillac

Herman Miller

Hewlett-Packard Company

H. J. Russell & Company

H.J.S. and Associates

Hodges Communications Group

Holiday Inn

Holland & Knight

Hollowell Foster & Gepp, P.C.

HomeBanc Mortgage Company

Horace Henry Photography

House of Seagram

Houston Digital Marketing

Hot 107.9

Hyatt Regency Atlanta Hotel

IBM

Ida Alice Ryan Charitable Trust

Illuminations

Immucor, Inc.

ING North America Insurance

Insights

International Sports & Entertainment
    Strategies

Jackmont Hospitality/Sodexho

JacksonHeath and Associates

JEMS Strategic Connections, Inc.

Jerry Thomas Arts-Africana

Jerzees Activewear

John H. Harland

John H. & Wilhelmina D. Harland
    Charitable Foundation

John & Mary Franklin Foundation

Johnny Walker

Johnson Controls

Johnson & Johnson Consumer
    Companies, Inc.

John Wieland Homes

J. P. Morgan Chase

Junior Achievement of Georgia

Kaiser Permanente

Kaplan, Inc.

Kappa Alpha Psi Fraternity (GSU)

Katherine John Murphy Foundation

KC Builders

Kendeda Fund

Kennesaw Lincoln Mercury

KFC Corporation

Khafra Engineering

King & Spalding

KISS 104.1

Korn/Ferry International

KPMG, LLP

Kroger Food Stores

Kuppenheimer Men's Clothiers

La-Van Hawkins InnerCity Foods/
    Checkers

LAZ Parking/Georgia, Inc.

Lincoln-Mercury

Lockheed Martin

Longhorn Steakhouse

Lowe's

Magic Johnson Theatres

Managed Healthcare Concepts, Inc.

MARTA

MARTA Employees Charity Club

Mary Allen Lindsey Branan
    Foundation

Mary Kay Cosmetics

Matlock & Associates

McBride Research Laboratories

McDonald's

MCI Telecommunications

McKenzie Funeral Home

Meharry Medical School

Meharry National Alumni
  Association

Mesirow Financial

MetLife Foundation

Metropolitan Atlanta Super Bowl
  XXXIV Host Committee

Metropolitan Life Insurance

MGR Food Services

Miller Brewing Company

Milliken

Mirant Corporation

Miss Marcile's Biscuits

Mizuno

Montier Designs

Morehouse College

Morehouse School of Medicine

Morris, Manning & Martin, LLP

MRI & Imaging of Georgia

Mrs. Winner's

Nabisco

National Arthritis Foundation

National Basketball Association

National Black College Alumni Hall
  of Fame   Foundation

National Center for Primary Care

National Football League

National Linen Service

National Mentoring Partnership

National Wildlife Federation

New Jomandi Productions

NFL Youth Education Town

Nike

Nokia

Northern Telecom

Norwest Contracting

O'Charley's

Omni Hotels

One Ninety One Peachtree
  Associates

Outdoor Systems, Inc.

Outward Bound Atlanta

Parke-Davis

Park Holdings, Inc. / Park'N Fly, Inc.

Parks & Crump, LLC

Patillo Construction Company

Pepsi-Cola Company

Pfizer, Inc.

Philip & Irene Toll Gage Foundation
  / Jim Cox, Jr. Foundation

Philips

Philips Consumer Electronics

Pillsbury

Pizza Hut-Bankhead Avenue

Polaroid Foundation

Porsche Cars North America

Praise 97.5

Price Gilbert, Jr. Charitable Fund

PriceWaterhouseCoopers

Prime Cable

Procter & Gamble

Production Dynamics of Atlanta

Prographics Communications, Inc.

Publix Super Markets Charities

Radio One Atlanta

Rainforest

Ralph From Ben Hill

Rare Hospitality

Ray M. & Mary Elizabeth Lee
    Foundation

R. D. Wood Insurance Associates

Red Rock Global

Remy Cointreau USA, Inc.

Renaissance Atlanta Hotel

Renaissance Cont. Co.

Residential Funding Group

Revlon

Rich's

Rio Mall

Ritz-Carlton Atlanta

Robert W. Woodruff Foundation

Rolling Out

Ross Laboratories

Royal Specialty Underwriting, Inc.

Royal Ten Cate USA

R.S. Thomas Training Associates

RTM Restaurant Group

Russell Athletic

Russell Corporation

Ryan Partnership/Pana Vista

Saks Fifth Avenue

Salomon Smith Barney

Samuel H. Archer Comprehensive

High School

SAVE

Schenley/Gordon's

Schieffelin & Somerset

SchlumbergerSema

Scholastic, Inc.

Scientific Visions

Sears

ServiceMaster Aviation

Shoneys

Siemens

Simon Schwob Foundation

Six Continents

Snapfinger Holdings

Solvay Pharmaceuticals

Sony Music Entertainment, Inc.

Soul Food Music Festival

South Carolina State University

South Fulton Running Partners

Southern Company

Southern Education Foundation

Southern Partners Fund

Southern University-Baton Rouge

Southwest Medical Center

Spartan Communications

Sports Marketing Services

Stanley, Love-Stanley, P.C.

Star Athletics

State Farm Foundation

State Farm Insurance Company

State of Georgia

Steelecase

Stouffer Renaissance Atlanta Hotel-
  Airport
SunTrust Foundation
Sweet Auburn Festival
Swift Services, Inc.
Synovus Financial Corporation
Ten Cate Nicolon, USA
Tenet Healthcare Foundation
Tenet Hospitals of Atlanta
Tennessee State University
Terry Manufacturing Company
The Atlanta Business Journal
The Atlanta Coca-Cola Bottling
  Company
The Atlanta Inquirer
The Atlanta History Center
The Atlanta Journal-Constitution
The Atlanta Project
The Atlanta Tribune
The Club of Hearts (Georgia Power)
The Coca-Cola Company
The Coca-Cola Foundation
The College Board
The Danner Foundation
The David, Helen and Marian
Woodward Fund
The Freemount Corporation
The GE Foundation
The GE Fund
The Ghana Expo
The Gillette Company
The Goizueta Foundation

The Home Depot
The Imlay Family Fund
The James M. Cox Foundation of
  Georgia, Inc.
The John H. and Wilhelmina D.
  Harland Charitable Foundation
The Kaufmann Clinic
The Lorac Group, Inc.
The Mall West End
The Rich Foundation
The Southland Corporation
The Symmetry Group
The Tyler Family Foundation
The UPS Foundation
The Varsity
The Wachovia Foundation
The Westin Peachtree Plaza Hotel
Ticketmaster
Toys R Us
TransAtlantic Imports
Tropicana
Tucker's Twins Worldwide Fitness
Tull Charitable Foundation
Turner Broadcasting System, Inc.
Turner South
Tyson Foods
UBS PaineWebber
United Airlines
United Food & Commerical Workers
  Union
United States Army
United States Coast Guard

United States Postal Service
Unity Jam
University of Georgia
University of Nebraska
UniverSoul Circus
UniWorld Group
UPN Atlanta
UPS
UPS Foundation
Upscale Magazine
U.S.A. Track & Field
V-103 FM
Verizon Foundation
Verizon Wireless
VF Corporation
Visions USA
Visual Solutions Graphic Design
Vitelcom Communications
VSA Arts
Wachovia Bank
Wal-Mart Corporation
Wal-Mart Foundation
WCLK Radio
West Fulton Middle School
West Paces Ferry Medical Center
WGCL-TV
WGNX-TV
Whelchel Wholistic Health Centre
Whitehall Foundation
Who's Who in Black Atlanta
WIGO Radio
William J. Scott Elementary School

William M. Boyd Elementary School
William Tolliver's Art Gallery, Inc.
WO&F
WTLK-TV
WXIA-TV / 11-Alive
WYZE Radio
Xerox of Georgia
Zakkee & Associates

AUTHOR'S NOTES

I am a Project Success Student, if I think back twenty-five years ago. I was born and raised in a little town called Rich Square, North Carolina in 1961. At age forty-four, my mother was a widow with ten children to raise.

Three months before graduating from high school in 1979, the Migrant Seasonal Farmers of North Carolina announced that they would send one student in each rural county of North Carolina to college on a full scholarship.

Many factors contributed to my name being placed in the selection process. My mother had little income and four children already in college. We all worked on the farm and I had been a member of the Future Farmers of America program at my high school for four years. I was also very involved in the community.

My English teacher Miss Rosa Adams, who had taught my mother and all of my siblings, called me into her office and said, "Moses, you are going to college free. All you have to do is keep your grades up and act like you got some home training."

Of all the students in Northampton County, I was the chosen one. God chose me.

That is my Project Success story. So, when John Grant came to me and asked me to write this book, I had no choice. I would only think of the quote "To whom much is given, much is required." I owe it to my God, Miss Adams, and the Migrant Seasonal Farmers of North Carolina to write this book. I owe it to the students of Project Success to tell their story, our story.

This is a book about courage. The courage of a group of men, who didn't have to do it, but they did anyhow. It is a love story. They loved children who needed to be loved.

When I started this book, I actually gave myself six months to complete this project. Those six months turned into two years after I rewrote the majority of the book because I realized I had made a mistake. The book was not about who is on the board, or who had the most mentees. It was standing face to face with the motive to do the right thing for the right reason; the children who the 100 Black Men of Atlanta had dared to make a difference in their lives. It is their story.

It is almost impossible to talk to them and not feel the love in their hearts for wanting a good education and a good life. One should understand that the children know what I knew twenty-five years ago. This is an opportunity for them to take the high road in life. It is their chance to be somebody.

So I am grateful to the 100 Black Men of Atlanta, Inc. because of their good deeds to the young. I would like to thank President Robert Haley, President elect Darrell Fitzgerald, William Stanley and COO, John T. Grant, Jr. and his staff for all that they do each day. A special thanks to Gayle L. Moses, Esquire and Karen D. Roberts, who stood by my side until the very end to make sure that book was published.

I am glad the 100 Black Men of Atlanta, Inc. stopped by Perry Homes all those years ago, the same way Miss Adams called me into her office. It is like the sound of a trumpet, but one has to be ready when it calls.

The students of Process Success are ready.

Shelia P. Moses

Author, playwright and producer, Shelia P. Moses has written several books including "The Legend of Buddy Bush" that awarded her as a finalist for the National Book Award and the Coretta Scott King Award. She also wrote Dick Gregory's memoirs, "Callus on My Soul," "I, Dred Scott," and "The Return of Buddy Bush." She is currently working on a documentary about Project Success and working on a book titled "I'm A Grady Baby." She resides in Atlanta, Georgia.

Photos from left to right above. *Row 1:* Juan D. Johnson • Khalil Johnson • Larry L. Johnson • Lonnie G. Johnson • Nathaniel Johnson, III, M.D. • Norman J. Johnson, Ph.D. • Roger D. Johnson • Milton H. Jones, Jr. • Milton V. Jones • Reuben D. Jones *Row 2:* Waymon E. Jones • Brian O. Jordan • T. Wayne Kauffman • Gregory A. Kearney, II • Charles J. Kelley • Henry A. Kelly • Albert L. Kemp, Esq. • Brian A. King, Sr. • William Lamar, Jr. • Ronny B. Lancaster *Row 3:* Joseph W. Larché, Jr. • Charles J. Lawson • Kenny L. Leon • Samuel L. Lott • Leroy Loving, Jr., M.D. • Ronald E. Mabra • Marvin C. Mangham, Jr. • James Martin • Walter E. Massey, Ph.D. • Carlton A. Masters *Row 4:* Cornell McBride, Sr. • William B. McQueen • Daniel R. Meachum, Esq. • Eugene Merriday • Albert C. Middleton • Larry J. Mims • Harold E. Mitchell, Sr. *Row 5:* Frank H. Monteith • Juan H. Montier, III • Charles W. Moore • Joseph L. Moore • Richard E. Moore, Ph.D. • Rodney G. Moore, Esq. • Sylvius S. Moore, Jr. • Donald K. Murphy • Kenneth E. Murray, Sr. • Edwin Neal *Row 6:* Robert L. Nibbs, Jr. • Edmund O. Nosegbe, C.P.A. • Bobby L. Olive • Michael R. Pack, P.E. • Kenneth D. Parks • Steven A. Patten, M.D. • Kenneth S. Payne • Dennis E. Pemberton, Jr. • Richard J. Pennington • Charles H. Petross *Row 7:* Charles O. Phillips, Ph.D. • Bernard M. Porché • Clarence Powell, Jr. • Kenneth A. Powell • Albenny Price, D.C. • Herman L. Reese, Ed.D. • Edward J. Renford • Derek K. Rhodes • Gary C. Richter, M.D. • Ray M. Robinson